From father to son

Vincenzo Berghella

Copyright Page

Copyright year: 2010

Copyright notice: by Vincenzo Berghella

All rights reserved

ISBN No: 978-0-578-13627-1

From the same author: (see also www.lulu.com)

- **Obstetric Evidence Based Guidelines.** Informa Healthcare, London, UK, and New York, USA (2007) [English]
- **Maternal Fetal Evidence Based Guidelines.** Informa Healthcare, London, UK, and New York, USA (2007)[English]
- **Laughter, the best medicine. Jokes for everyone.** (2007) [English]
- **Ridere, la migliore medicina. Barzellette per bambini.** (2007) [Italiano]
- **My favorite quotes.** (2009) [English]
- **In medio stat virtus – Citazioni d'autore.** (2009) [Italiano]
- **Quello che di voi vive in me.** (2009) [Italiano]
- **Dall'altra parte dell'oceano.** (2010) [Italiano] [Translated in: **On the other side of the ocean.** (2013) [English]
- **Preterm Birth: Prevention and Management.** Wiley-Blackwell. Oxford, United Kingdom. (2010) [English]
- **From father to son.** (2010) [English]
- **Sollazzi.** (2010) [Italiano]

- **The land of religions.** (2011) [English] [Translated in: **La terra delle religioni.** (2013) [Italiano]
- **Giramondo.** (2011) [Italiano]
- **Obstetric Evidence Based Guidelines.** Informa Healthcare, London, UK, and New York, USA (2012; Second Edition) [English]
- **Maternal Fetal Evidence Based Guidelines.** Informa Healthcare, London, UK, and New York, USA (2012; Second Edition) [English]
- **Trip to London.** (2012) [English]
- **Il primo amore non si scorda mai.** (2012) [Italiano]
- **Maldives.** (2013) [English]
- **Russia.** (2013) [English]
- **Happiness: the scientific path to achieving well-being.** (2014) [English]

Index

9	Introduction
13	From me to you
18	Universal Commandments
26	Life is a wonderful thing
29	Do what you like to do
32	Discover yourself
34	Be yourself
37	Continue to improve yourself
47	The school of life
52	Work hard
61	Play hard
63	Girls
65	Life-long partner
71	Family
72	Children
78	Friends
81	Communicate
84	Keep in shape
88	Money
91	Religion
103	Country
106	Count on me
108	Conclusion

To my sons Andrea and Pietro,
and all the sons and daughters of the world

Introduction

Putting one foot in front of the other can be improved by knowing better the path in front of you.

Life is a wonderful experience. But it can be challenging, difficult. You will have to make a lot of decisions along the way. Quality of existence depends on the choices one makes. Experience helps you avoid mistakes, making life less arduous. I've often said that I would buy experience if it was for sale.

For young women and men of the world, know-how is in the future, and life must be lived initially without it. There is no substitution for skill acquired in your own skin.

Nonetheless, I feel that my experience should be helpful to my kids. I've always looked at my parents as two people whom I could learn from. I knew their place in life well. How did they get there? By knowing their experience, their values, I could start from a higher point than just bare zero.

Every time an old man or woman dies, it's as if a library went up in flames. The library that we have accumulated during life should be left for the next lives to enjoy, as they wish. Common human conditions affect every man and woman, and we can all learn from each other.

Thank you Andrea and Pietro for the great privilege and for the immense pleasure of being your father. You each have 50% of my DNA. So I want to pass on some lessons I've learned along the way of these first 45 years of my life. Behavior often follows habits, and forming good habits when young, as soon as possible, will ease them into your life.

I am a father, not a mother. As my wife Paola said, 'I failed twice', meaning I fathered two sons, and no daughter. Nonetheless, this book is in general from a parent to his child. While my own experience has been from 'father to son', I think women can certainly share the vast majority of the thoughts in this volume.

I've given in this book some examples from my life, but, mostly, I have given general principles. You the reader should interpret the instructions according to your own life episodes and condition. From these lessons form your own philosophy of life.

Vincenzo Berghella

From me to you

Life must be lived going forward,
but can be understood only going backward.
Kierkegaard

June 1997
Dear Andrea,
it's 7pm, a beautiful evening in June. There are 33 years between us. You were not around these first 33 years of my life. I want to tell you some stories from my experiences so far.

Life is a wonderful thing, and you'll see reading these pages how much I have enjoyed. Life is also full of events and responsibilities that one can better deal with if helped by someone you love, someone you can trust, someone who has more experience than you and has already gone down the road of life.

You are just a 16 week fetus. Happy 16th week today! You are my first (I hope) son. I wish that one day, maybe when you are 33 years old, you also will be happy with your life, also thanks to the relationship you have had with me and your mother Paola, thanks to what she and I have passed on to you.

The reason for this book, or at least the excuse I came up with, is narrating to you the experiences I've had so far. What I've learned from my existence. The first part of life, up to 4-5 years old, you will forget. Then, up to 10-12 years old, you will spend most of your time playing. But in these first years, your most important values will develop.

Then comes the delicate time of middle school and high school. And after that, the years of college and perhaps graduate school, where a person who up to then has been just 'potential', finally 'forms' himself and becomes a teacher, a blacksmith, a lawyer, a husband, a bum, a father.

I hope to make you understand through the pages of this book what I've learned in my life. How events have interacted with the different facets of my personality. I consider myself happy and content, often carefree. Sometimes it appears that I can't stop kidding around. But the ones who know me well are familiar with other sides of me.

Today (33 years, 4 months), I'm an accomplished physician. I have made the choice of coming to study and then work in the United States. I have studied hard in 2 different languages, 2 diverse continents. I'm a professor, I teach, I study the fetus and complications of pregnancy. I've married a wonderful woman, your mother, who for sure has transmitted to you the best parts of your DNA.

Without more boasting, I just want to say that I've had to choose, to make important decisions, and that making them has at times not been easy. Not at all. I feel like every day I have to make many important evaluations. The more I advance in life, the more responsibility, the more influence I have. The older I get, the more I understand the important consequences that my actions have not just for me, but also for others.

I do not want to lose the opportunity to pass on what I have learned to you. For me, the person who I love and trust, and who has had more experience than me going down the road of life is <u>my father</u>. His name is also Andrea, like yours. He has also had always 33 years more than me. I have seen in him a model to follow for many reasons. He had built for him and for us, his family, a serene environment, with the certainty that possible future clouds either would not come or would be easily confronted, thanks to him, without any problem. He has given us tranquility, as we knew we could always count on him.

My father, your homonymous grandfather, is a very extroverted man, at the center of any discussion he's involved in. But, perhaps because I moved to the USA when I was just 19, he has not had the opportunity, or felt the necessity, to tell me much about his own story. Only now, as we both get older, he has opened up, and begins to recount not just the stories, but how he felt about those stories, and what he learned from the path of his existence.

I want to tell you my stories early, instead. So you can make use of them, if you want. The first 20 years of life you make extremely important choices, which will affect the rest of your life. You'll make them without much practice in life. To do well, one must practice. In life, experience is key. If it was on sale, the smart ones would buy it, at any price. Even when you have some experience, you seek more. You seek experience from someone else, a magazine, a book, a friend, a relative. As you grow up, you'll see how much you have in common with the members of your family. Even if your life will be different than your ancestors, you'll see the similarities in DNA. Aspects of your character, of your feelings, of your manias and of your doubts, come from them.

When faced with different choices, you'll ask yourself: "What would grandpa have done in this situation? What would mother have done? What would father have considered?" So many questions: "What school should I attend? What sport to practice? What friends to associate with? Which girls to court? What should I do when I grow up? How do I respond to a reproach, to a swear, to an injustice? What's honesty? Love? How do I behave in these situations? Who am I?"

Dear son, do not misunderstand me. I do not want a clone of our ancestors, or, even less, a clone of myself. I just want to donate you my experience. Which is tied to the experiences of my family and of the ones who have crossed my path, from whom I've learned myself.

I've always loved biographies. And history books. In these scripts, you get to know the end. Napoleon took a decision, and now, given its consequence and 'the future' which followed that decision, you know if that decision was 'good' or 'bad'. Right, or wrong. That's why they make you study Napoleon.

But Napoleon was a short French man who lived more than 200 years ago. I believe that you can learn from anyone's experience, but the experience of your immediate relatives is the one in which you'll recognize yourself the most. First of all, as I just said, at least certain aspects of your character will be similar to some relative. Many have lived in your times. Often geographically they have lives in similar surroundings. So it's probable that they have had to face situations that you'll face in the future, in this new millennium about to start.

The difference is that you know the outcome, the consequences of their actions. You, instead, must decide one specific day whether to court this or that other girl, or even whether to marry her forever, having no idea if you'll be happy with her. If that is the right decision, or the wrong one. Or if there is a better one.

Your decision of course is yours to make. And you'll ponder her character, intelligence, beauty (inside and outside), and a thousand of other factors, including the 'timing'. But I think that, in your intricate reflections of those moments, you'll consider also other 'data': "My friend Joe married Simona and is happy, how come…? My friend Ilaria married Frank and is unhappy, how come…?" And so on.

Often, you'll wonder, consciously or unconsciously: "What did dad find in mom that convinced him to court her and then to stay with her for so long? What are the characteristics that make them a good match? Why did 'nonna' stay more than 50 years with 'nonno'? What made that possible? What is the secret of their bond?"

Some things will be obvious, and you'll need no explanations from the persons involved. You know why some things have happened. You have formed your truth. But, often, you feel like asking the protagonists of the story you are pondering: "Why did you do this? How did you get to this point?"

Let me tell you up front a suggestion: do not judge persons or facts superficially. The world is full of false news, of fictitious 'facts'. Only the eye-witnesses know the facts. Often nobody wants to talk about a sin, a misdeed. But you come from an honest, very honest family.

If you ask us, we'll tell you the truth. The experiences, in detail, as they happened. The triumphs. The errors. The stories of your family among wars, loves, births, deaths, successes, failures, money or poverty, wisdom and madness.

Universal commandments

Wisdom is not a product of schooling but of the lifelong attempt to acquire it.
Albert Einstein

Think with your own mind. Make decisions after knowing the facts and getting advice, but, in the end, it's you who should decide based on your best judgment. Do not let external events or people influence your mind or your actions excessively.

Be honest. A life built on cheating will crumble sooner or later. And even if nobody else notices you have not been truthful, you have! And you are the one who has to live with the remorse. True delight comes from an achievement accomplished fairly.

Love. Expressing your affection towards others will make you feel great. Love given makes two people more sturdy: both the giver and the receiver. Love is contagious. Kiss, embrace, touch. We are too stingy with expressing our affections.

Keep a good rapport with everyone. Give respect before you expect it. Treat people the way you want to be treated. Be the first to set the good example. Remember, any other human being is genetically 99.9% exactly as you. Do not let the 0.1% difference blind you to all the other good.

Be altruistic. By securing the good of others, you secure your own good. Care, give, protect the weak, feed the hungry, comfort the desperate. Provide charity for all. Hell is realizing that you could have helped, but did not.

To give is better than to receive. Many feel they get strong by receiving (love, presents, attention, etc). Try to feel strong by giving (love, presents, attention, etc). The smiles you'll cause by giving will produce your most profound joy.

Avoid making enemies. Having an enemy can ruin your serenity. It's better to prevent one foe than to make a friend. Hatred is the worst affliction. Do not hate anyone. Never, ever get angry, especially in public.

Be sincere. When you say what happened frankly, and especially what you think genuinely, you move the world towards a better place, not backward. Be loyal to and cultivate those who foster truthfulness. Do not be or be around hypocrites.

Hard work, responsibility, duty: seek them gladly. Embrace sacrifice for a good cause. Serve. Sacrifice if needed. Do not get used to being served.

Be positive. Being optimistic and seeing the encouraging side of things will make you a better person. Concentrate on the good. Focus on the half full part of the glass, not on the half empty. Look forward to the future with a smile.

Be a good example. Seneca, the Roman writer, said that the road of sermons is long, while the road of example short and efficacious. You do not have to say as much when your actions point to the wise road.

The truth often lies in the middle, not at the extremes. Extreme views to the left, or the right, and the inability to consider the good parts of other arguments, are wrong, and sterile. They do not move you closer to the reality. Choose a candidate, a friend, a colleague not because of the flag they wave, but because of the fact they have principles, and goals, that you also embrace.

Do not take sides forever. Adhering to an idea, a party, a cause, does not mean you have to follow it to extremes you disagree with.

Your health is a most precious commodity. Take care of yourself. The more active you stay (at work, at home, everywhere), the healthier you'll be. Without your good health, as well as the health of the ones you care for, it's hard to get to anything else.

Family is where your home and comfort are and will be. Cherish the family members you acquired when you were born. Form a new family to donate your love to, and pass on your own teachings.

Find friends you can tell your most inner secrets to, so they can help you cope with life's difficulties. Finding a good friend is like finding a treasure. Cultivate the handful of true friends you can trust.

Read a lot. It will open your mind to new ideas. And it will help you discover the world. You'll figure out what in the world you like best. Read everything, especially what you think can improve you, voraciously.

Travel. You'll discover what was described as different and therefore 'evil' is actually quite interesting and acceptable. Being exposed to the new will give you a chance to choose if that 'new' can improve yourself or your life.

Proceed through life calmly, without rushing. Maintain your cool. Sometimes there'll be confusion, and noise, around you. Don't let them affect you.

Believe in God. Do not be a religious fanatic. Creeds of all religions are about the same, such as helping others, not committing murder, or theft. Follow these general standards not just because you belong to a sect, but because they are the right life principles on which to base a successful and happy existence.

Love the world. Earth is a great place to live in. Make sure you do your best to preserve it, and perhaps even improve it. Adopt a 'green' lifestyle which respects the soil, the natural resources, animals, plants, everything that is nature.

Be confident. And be unpretentious. You may not be the best. But be aware that we do not live in a world of giants. Even the leader, the President of the United States, or whomever is the person you most admire, is full of faults, of shortcomings.

State your opinion with composed clarity during conversations. Ponder your words carefully. Do not follow the majority opinion just to be safe. When you disagree, do not say so. Say something like: "I see things differently." Or: "There is something else we can consider." Do not let a small disagreement ruin a great relationship.

If you can, cite data to confirm the scientific nature of your opinion, based on facts. Your audience will be impressed, and, most importantly, more likely to move towards your suggestion. If you look for them, there are figures and information for almost all issues. Make sure to know them if the matter is of importance to you.

Make sure to listen to others. You will learn a lot. And often your silence will be perceived like intelligence. People like to be listened to. They will be thankful of your listening, and be happy of your patience and attentiveness. Everybody has an interesting story to tell. You can learn something from almost anybody.

Be a good listener. Really listen, especially when you hear wisdom. And do not be afraid to keep quiet. Sometimes people think you are smart more by keeping your mouth closed than by opening it and saying something just to break the silence, letting them become aware of your shortcomings.

Learn from others. This is just my story, the story of one man. Even if I've studied all my life, I know so little. I've only one very narrow vision. I know very little about how to make an atomic bomb, life in Mongolia, the Arabic language. Or about airspace engineering. You can learn so much from others! Often quicker than you can learn from books, if the person is wise and erudite.

Be nice to nerds. To introverted geniuses. To the best in the class who is getting teased. It's very possible you'll end up working for them one day. You will often learn more from the quiet ones than from the verbose.

Avoid persons who are vulgar, arrogant, obtuse. They are a waste of time, and can ruin your mood, your spirit, your life. Do not let them interfere with your gladness and torment you. Mixing with them gives them strength and weakens you.

You will have to trust some people. In general, your doctor will operate on the side of your body that is sick. The cleaning lady will make your house shine. The priest will teach universal good values.

Unfortunately though, you can really only trust yourself. If you are lucky, you will be able to trust the good faith of your wife, your kids, your parents and family. But even they, with good intentions, can fail you. This is one of the saddest truths of life, and you better learn it soon. Sometimes, to know the truth, you have to listen to two liars. That's why it's good to get as much information as you can.

<u>Be humble</u>. Only idiots think theirs is the single right opinion. If you have nothing smart to say, remain quiet. Socrates smartly said that the more you know, the more you do not know.

<u>Avoid violence</u> at all costs. I have never been in a fight. I am still ashamed that, when I was about 15, I gave one light punch to the back of a friend of mine while playing soccer (I forgot the reason why). He turned, and looked at me surprised. He never said a word, and did not hit me in return. I am still mortified of that unique episode of my life. Never fight physically, there is nothing to gain.

<u>If it feels wrong, don't do it</u>. Stay away from the bad. Avoid the immoral, the corrupt, the wicked, the cruel, the merciless.

<u>Be fair</u>. Do not take advantage of others. You do not want people to 'bend' inappropriately for you, as much as you do not want to bend for people when unacceptable.

<u>Be careful when judging</u>. When you give your opinion, know the facts. Do not rush into judgment before you have obtained as much information and heard as many witnesses as possible. Do we ever really know the people we judge? Most of the times there is a reason for what we believe to be 'bad' behaviors in others. At least, before labeling someone as unjust, learn the facts. Even then, it's almost impossible to really know the truth. Accept others as they are. Do not be too judgmental. You do not know others' circumstances, their past.

<u>Do not judge only with today's eyes what has happened yesterday</u>. Yesterday's situation, values, relationships, and other variables might have been entirely different. I struggle and suffer when I see a good couple split. Stereotypical, superficial judgments make us say: "It was his fault," or "It was her fault." Or even: "The responsibility of the separation between two people is always fifty-fifty." Well, all these are labels that are often wrong.

<u>Force yourself to judge less</u>, and help more. That is what counselors do. They do not want to quickly apply blame on someone. They need hours, weeks, months of investigation to find patterns in the relationship that lead to friction and disagreements. Only then can they be helpful. And they cannot help if they listen to only one side.

<u>Be sincere with others, even when it's not easy, or even painful.</u> Many friends, who genuinely want to help, reinforce beliefs in one member of the split couple which are not completely true. This behavior makes the separation and the anguish of their friend even deeper.

<u>Be a good friend</u>. As an example, I struggled over 11 years to find the right girl to spend the rest of my life happily with. Tonino, my friend since high school, told me that my struggle was not due to the fact that I had not found the right girl. I was the problem. I was not mature enough for a long-lasting relationship. I was too flirty, too quickly bored. I could have met the best girl for me in the world, and still dumped her within months. I was the culprit. This straight and sincere counseling is what friends are for.

<u>Underpromise, and overdeliver</u>, both to yourself, as well as others. Try to underestimate the reward. To assure to others that you will achieve a goal while you can't be sure, will make you look foolish when the objective is not reached. So be careful, and promise little, dedicating your efforts to eventually being able to give more than the others expect.

<u>Be a leader</u>. Lead by example, not fear. It's important to responsibly show the way. Choose the team you lead carefully, making sure it's made of champions.

<u>Believe in others</u>. I believe that there is a natural instinct for man to be good. Sometimes bad examples, or often harsh episodes during formative years, make some people immoral, or cruel. But almost always, masked behind such behaviors, the basic instinct is for decency, kindness, altruism in the right circumstances.

<u>Learn from people who think like you, but even more from those with different beliefs</u>. Often you learn the right way by seeing others going the wrong way.

<u>Be patient</u>. Time often fixes things. If you do not get promoted today, you probably will tomorrow. Speeding with a car or any motorized vehicle is dangerous, and saving a few minutes won't change the outcome majorly. Be on time by starting on time, not by rushing.

<u>Time is one of the most precious commodities</u>. Not only in terms of lifespan. Especially when you have to make an important choice (wife, job, house, etc), make sure you take your time. Time is often more important than money (and it also helps make it).

<u>Start saving early</u>. If you, beginning at 25 years old, save $1,000 per year and it makes 8% in interest, when you are 65 it'll be worth $386,506. If you start doing the same when you are 35, you'll have $172,317. That $10,000 you have not invested between 20 and 30 has 'cost' you over $200,000. This is the miracle of compounding interest.

<u>Be careful what you wish for</u>. Be aware that sometimes not getting what you want may be a wonderful stroke of luck, as said by the Dalai Lama. When I did not get a prestigious grant from the National Institute of Health, I was able to write books, both scientific and non-fiction, that I would have never had the time to write if I had gotten the grant.

<u>Dress well</u>. People get a first impression of someone (or even something) in the first minute. If your hair is uncombed, your clothing disheveled, your fly open, you can be saying lots of intelligent things, but the impression will still not be positive.

<u>Be clean, with hair neatly kept, and appropriate clothing</u>. At work, for a guy, it's easy. A white shirt, a blue jacket, gray pants. When you are young, blue or grey pants, and a white or light blue shirt are perfect. You cannot go wrong. Shoes can be black, with laces or moccasins, with black belt. Women, both young and old, will love you for this.

It's bad to follow the current fashion. That's invented just to sell clothes to people who have already plenty of them. There is no need for what you wear to be made by famous or trendy artists. There is no need to appease external forces to dress in the latest style. In fact, once in a while, it's good to show off with something unique to you, that shows your personality or your mood of the moment.

Accept change wisely. Change is good when it does not interfere with your core values. Usually, it's not wise to be the first, or the last, to accept the new. For example, in medicine you want to begin to think about adopting a new intervention when at least two large, well done studies have been published. The same in life.

Life is a wonderful thing

The best way to make children good is to make them happy.
Oscar Wilde

<u>Consider yourself lucky</u>. A positive attitude makes you more successful. You'll get a job, a girl, a friend because you smile. If you are down, feel sorry for yourself, or keep a frown on your face, nobody wants to give you a chance. You'll be passed over.

<u>Smile, it's contagious</u>. People want to be around happy people. You at least must be the one to like yourself and your life, and show it to others with a positive attitude. Those that criticize their life and their choices, criticize themselves, and basically admit they are not worth much.

<u>Enjoy every period of your life</u>. Each one has his advantages. Do not long for the past, or hope for a better tomorrow without working for it. Every day is a present: that is why it is called the 'present'. Make the most of it. Carpe diem. Make sure you do the juvenile things when you are young.

The classic example is girls. Make sure you meet and go out enough before getting married. The period you date girls is before you marry and have kids, not after. It's easier not to want back a certain phase of your life if you have enjoyed the characteristics of that period. The same can be said of not being too serious when you are a child. Make sure you have some fun.

<u>You count a lot</u>. You may not realize it yet, but your young life is extremely important for many people. Watch 'It's a wonderful life,' the movie with James Stewart where an angel makes him realize how many people would have suffered and whose life would have been turned for the worse if he was never born. Count your blessings.

<u>It's better to peak in life later, than when you are very young</u>. It's hard not to get depressed later if you achieve fame and fortune before 20 years of age. It's hard to live up to early success. The rule of regression to the mean will probably balance your life back

closer to the average, and you risk early disappointment and depression. That does not mean you should not go for high goals whenever you want.

Life is full of opportunities. Take them. In fact, the worst thing is to pass up opportunities that you regret not taking. You will have many trains of chances pass by. Evaluate them carefully, and take the ones you believe in. Life cannot be lived watching all trains go by you. Jump on some. Don't follow trends, but take the opportunity that is best for you. And remember that you won't find something unless you look for it. Sometimes the train does not come to you, you have to seek it.

When in front of the sea, you can either just watch it, or go out and explore it, conquer it, discover it. Be the one able to go out at sea, and come back alive and improved, having enhanced it. Some people just drift through life. They are afraid of both life and death. Be courageous. Do not be afraid.

I admire activity. I must admit I do not care much for those who just like to criticize. You will be remembered by what you build, not by what you destroy. I have high regard for the human being who does, who tries, whose face is covered by dust, sweat and blood, who strives valiantly. In the end, this brave being will either know the triumph of high achievement, or at the worst, if he fails, at least he will know that he not just been a spectator in life, but that he has tried and dared greatly.

Life is a challenge at times. It will get you hurt. If you do not want to fail, do nothing. Stay there in front of the TV. I promise you'll regret it, and be ashamed of your life when you ponder its significance. You must be able to accept the bad times, as they are there to enhance the feeling of the good times. Life can be unfair. Better get used to it. As your grandmother used to say, when a door closes, a bigger one opens. Be ready for the next chance, without feeling sorry for the one missed.

It's wonderful to earn rewards with your own hard work and dedication. Your boss will be harsher than your teacher. That is why your mother and I do not give you everything you want. Life won't either. You have to earn it. Expecting everything to be due to you is the best step towards complete failure. The world expects you to do something before you merit recompense.

<u>Competition is good</u>. Compare yourself to the best, not the worst. In your school it might not look at times that there are the best and the worst. They do not use grades. But your boss will. Everyone will judge you, and those judgments will affect every step of your existence. Be prepared to shine by giving your best.

<u>Do not blame others for your mistakes</u>. It's easy to blame parents, teachers, friends, colleagues, or just bad luck. Be aware of your own shortcomings. It's the only way to improve, and win when you get another chance.

<u>Be kind</u>. Hug people, let the ones you love feel it. Be affectionate with the ones you care for. Let women go first through the door. Help the needy. Support the old and weak.

<u>Be thankful</u>. Enjoy all of life. Including what you might take for granted. Many nights I go to sleep being thankful because I had water to drink when I was thirsty. Because I had food when I was hungry. Because I could sleep 8 hours when my eyes felt like closing after a long day of duty.

Strive for <u>moments that will take your breath away</u> because of beauty, happiness, and achievement. It's not how many breaths you take, but what happens when you are breathing. A long, empty, meaningless life can be pure torture, and lead to depression and misery.

Do what you like to do

The future belongs to those who believe in the beauty of their dreams.
                              Eleanor Roosevelt

Follow your dreams. Be a dreamer, go for your goals, don't get lazy. You will see that your dreams will change, but the biggest, most basic ones, usually stay the same. Do not let go until you achieve your goals. Try to get what you love, otherwise you'll have to settle for loving what you get.

Choose you profession wisely, according to your characteristics and your long-term dreams. It does not matter what you do. As long as you do it to the best of your abilities. Any occupation can be worthy when done with love and dedication. Any career can make the world better if done with humility, devotion, and enthusiasm.

As with choosing a mate, choosing a profession that will make you satisfied requires being exposed to as many occupations as possible. Examine the jobs and ask about the life situations of your parents' friends. Visit factories, fields, professional offices, restaurants, shops, any place where people work, so as to evaluate if you can see yourself doing that for 40 plus years.

Choose something that excites you. Do not choose something you can do. Select something that will challenge you. That will not bore you. That you think has value for you, for your family, but also for society at large, even for humanity.

Only by trying different experiences will you know what's best for you. My academic career path culminated in becoming Chairman. I did not enjoy the administrative part of medicine. A situation where health and economics dangerously mix. So I declined to take the permanent position. And I chose instead to pursue quality in clinical care, education, and research. These are the activities I absolutely adore in medicine. I evolved into knowing this is what I liked, discovering myself through challenges.

<u>Maintain interest in your profession</u>. Try to excel at it. To be one of the best at a particular aspect of your work. Especially the parts you enjoy the most. Do not get dragged into doing what you do not enjoy. Make sure your profession continues to challenge you. Avoid boredom at work.

<u>Have goals in life</u>. Love for improving mankind. Finding a good companion. One who is trustworthy, and complimentary to you. Do things you like to do, not necessarily those for which you get external praise. Judge what you obtained in relation to what you gave up for it. Even better, try to calculate what you risk losing BEFORE deciding to attack the next challenge.

<u>Have somebody to look up to and imitate</u>. Often part of your dream is to emulate your heroes. I wanted to be as honest and as hard working as my dad. I wanted to be as nice to people as some of my colleagues. I wanted to be as available as others as some of my friends. Nobody will be the perfect package to imitate in entirety, but you can make a wonderful puzzle of yourself by following the superior pieces of worthy examples.

<u>Without risking failure, there is little chance of success</u>. If you believe in the goal, follow it. The beginning is always the toughest part. Years from now, you'll be disappointed usually not for what you did, but for what you did not do. One day, when you are looking back at your life, and even today, you might already be more disappointed by the things you did not do, than by those you did do.

So, as Mark Twain said, "<u>throw off your bowlines</u>. Sail away from the safe harbor. Catch the trade winds in your sail." You are a ship, and ships were not made to stay in the harbor. A man who follows his dreams is a happy man. And the only one with a chance of making his dreams come true. The future belongs to you if you believe in the possibility of your dreams.

Some have liked that they knew even when they were little where they would die, and even who would bury them. I have lived differently, worrying a lot more about living than preparing for death. The main preparation for death has been to '<u>check' my dreams, to make them happen and check them as 'done' on my mental agenda,</u> before it was too late. And I made sure to feel like it was never too late. If going to Machu Picchu came around, and I had time and money, I went.

<u>Balance is important</u>. "Keep your eyes on the stars and your feet on the ground," as said by President Theodore Roosevelt, seems like good advice to me.

Discover yourself

There is only one journey. Going inside yourself.
Rainer Maria Rilke

γνωθι σεαυτόν : "Discover yourself" in ancient Greek. This was inscribed at the lintel of the entrance to the Temple of Apollo at Delphi. Your life will be happy and gratifying if you learn who you are, what you want, what your values and goals are.

Discovering yourself is the hardest trip you'll have to take. Especially when you are young. You have not yet been tested. Life will put you in situations in which cheating is possible, and perhaps very advantageous. And in other circumstances where you will have the opportunity to be kind to people, if you so choose. Your true self is the latter.

You'll be lucky if you discover early in life what you like. Often it's difficult to do. My cousin Carlo liked to play with model cars when he was a child. He kept it going, with passion and wisdom. He developed an organized collection when he was a teenager. He repaired them, cleaned them, never lost one. He is now one of the biggest model car dealers in the world (www.carmodel.com).

Try to find your path before your 21st or 22nd birthday. Great ideas come to those younger than 25, 30, usually. Try to make best use of your mind and body when 18 to 30. This is when you have the best energies, still pure, rough and still capable of all functions, inventions, ideas, undertakings.

Success often comes in your 20's. Einstein discovered the theory of relativity when he was 25 years old. Mozart composed his first opera at 14. DeBakey invented the pump for the artificial heart at 23. Hannibal defeated the Romans in Cannes at 27. Watson discovered the structure of DNA at 24. This list could continue for a long time. After 30 you can certainly have significant achievements. The best successes then are a good spouse and healthy kids.

<u>You have to learn who you are. Most importantly, what makes you happy.</u> If you seek happiness, first you have to understand the causes that give rise to it, what events make you happy. As importantly, happiness also means not being unhappy, so in addition you must discover what makes you suffer. Then you need to search events that make you content, and avoid those that cause you pain.

<u>Dance to the music that comes from within</u>. Or at least dance to music you have chosen. Do not just follow trends, fashion, other people's choices without before forming your own. Follow your core. Be a first rate version of yourself, not a second copy of someone else. Pretend to be you, and be careful about what you pretend. Truth lies within you.

<u>Self-neglect is as bad</u>, or maybe worse, than selfishness. Remember to concentrate on yourself and what you are. Many others will pull in different directions, at school, at work, at home, while you play. Respecting yourself you will be able to then respect others. Only once you know and love yourself, can you know and love others.

Be yourself

Do not change your core self; follow it.

<u>Be yourself</u>. Do not pretend to be someone else. If you are not tough, do not pretend to be. If you are not good at something, do not boast your talents. Sooner or later the truth will be evident to all. If you are effeminate, let that part out, do not suppress it. If you like sports, play them. If you like to lead, try to. If you do not, be content to follow the pack and contribute in other ways.

Once you have <u>your values, your dreams, your taste</u> for certain things, follow them. Only do what your heart tells you to do. You will be an outstanding, positive human being once you can say what you think, not what others want you to say. <u>Do not be afraid to voice your opinion</u>.

Nonna Tita, my mother, used to tell me: "Pensa sempre con la tua testa," meaning <u>"Always think with your own head."</u> Do listen to others, but form your opinion according to what your intelligence is telling you. This is perhaps the best teaching I have ever received.

<u>Do not side yourself necessarily with a party</u>. Vote the single issue. Choose the ideals. Cast the ballot with your own conscience, not following what this or that club, president, or party wants you to. I have been a democrat, a republican, and an independent, depending on who was the candidate in whom I most saw my values. Do not sell your brain to a banner for life.

<u>Do not be externally directed</u>. You'll become someone else, not yourself. Learn to be internally directed, to follow your ideals. Hopefully, by the time you learn to self-direct yourself in your daily life, you'll have acquired the best values to stir your compass. This concept is well described by Elisa Medhus in "Kids who think by themselves."

Despite the stress of choices, duties, responsibilities, <u>stay in peace with your soul</u>. You won't be able to live with yourself if you betray these inner core principles. You'll regret cheating for the rest of your life. You won't lament broken dreams if you tried to follow them.

Life is about the pursuit of happiness. I have discovered that happiness has different meanings for different people. My happiness comes from being around people I love and admire. Working hard at work worth doing, because it betters both the individual and humanity. Small things such as drinking clean fresh water when I'm thirsty delight me. Whatever it is you like and has value, chase it.

Do not pretend feelings. If you do not love your companion, tell her/him. They will suffer more later if you simulate a sentiment that has changed. At times when young I've tried to fake love: it's impossible. And unfair for your friend.

So how do you 'be yourself'? I can give you my example, which obviously I know best. I hope it is helpful. It has taken me years of introspection to understand myself.

I did not mind when I was young being a 'nerd', or a guy who does a lot of school work. I still don't mind working hard, often 60-70 hours per week. I still do not care what others think of me regarding my dedication. If it is for a good cause, in my case improving the lives and health of mothers and babies (and therefore their families), then this ardor is a blessing. Caring for the sick is a stroke of luck. Walking in a hospital and knowing I'll be able to help makes me feel worthy.

For me, to look a fool is the secret of a wise man, as said by Edgar Allan Poe, and posted on the wall of Café Reggio, in Manhattan, New York. I have always been an 'A' student, and my commitment to excellence continued in my medical work. But that does not mean that I cannot be a joker when the situation allows it. Humor heals, too. Laugher is a great medicine, and helps the rapport with others.

Follow your own Reason. Be someone you would be proud of. Do not be just like me, but, just like me, be yourself. I have the impression many people make up their personality. They pretend to be someone. That someone may be a bully, a fashionista, a tough lawyer, an apparently nice girl, etc. But often what they are pretending is not really who they are.

Sometimes people are afraid to say they do not like a dress, a song, a city, a movie, a house, just because everybody else before them has said they love it. Do not be afraid to sing outside the chorus, occasionally. Let others know what you really like.

If people know what you really like, they will invite you to do more of it. My friends invite me to soccer. The fact that finally, at 44 years old, I put a picture of myself playing soccer in a medical lecture at our annual national meeting in front of thousands of doctors, earned me praise, envy, and an invitation to lecture at distinguished universities. The Italian Consulate has invited me to captain their soccer team.

Do not pretend to like what you don't. You'll be invited to do it again and again, and find yourself in despair.

Continue to improve yourself

Be the change you want to be.
                              Mahatma Gandhi

May 24, 2010

Dear Pietro,

Since you were 2-3 years old, I have been seeing myself through you. You have innate happiness to live, to just be. You sing incessantly. At home or in the car, when us 4 family members pause talking, we can hear you humming away. You vocalize your well-being, your serenity. You recite known songs, but mostly make up new ones.

We parents often see ourselves in our children. I hope you will do the same with yours, one day. But we are also all unique. I'm happy you have my way of being carefree, of seeing life as something positive, wonderful. You love to dance like I do, you like to party. Perhaps because you are the second child, you are more relaxed than I am. Everyone likes you.

I wonder how you, and people and events around you, will influence your future development after these first 10 years. I hope you will read more, and find passion in some endeavor other than video games. Your mother, I, and your teachers are extremely impressed by your precise memory, your sharp eyesight, your mathematical skills, your social abilities.

You have amazing talents. Despite being my son, you are neat. You know already how to fold shirts and pants better than I ever did. You have powerful arms, bigger than mine, and your strong shoulders, while probably inherited from me, are straighter and broader than mine. You are at the 95 percentile for all body measurements we have taken so far.

You have a determined temperament. You love thrills. One of the games we play demonstrates your predilection for exciting stimulants. You stand on our king bed, and let me take your feet from under you, so you fall on your back like dead weight. When I did put you upside down as a child, you loved the ecstasy of this buzz. I hope you'll learn to control yourself. Some experiences are dangerous to your health.

Every child is special, and with every child one has a special relationship. Just like my mother felt a special relationship with me, given similar romantic and sensitive traits, I do feel the same with you. We are fortunate we communicate well. You and Andrea talk all the time, probably even more than your mother and I. Andrea has also an open heart and mind with us immediate family members. It's a feeling of trust that makes our lives full, not lonely as they could be.

I hope you will also control your appetite for other things, such as food. We tend to grow love handles around our waist, you and I. Feeling lean and healthy is something your mother and I are actively trying to teach you. You bear the name of your wonderful maternal grandparent, and have to uphold his great example of honesty and selflessness. Thank you for being Pietro Berghella. You are certainly already a wonderful human being, whom I admire. Use your talents well.

I'll always be with you, and root for you,
Papa'

Build yourself. You have a set of genes which you cannot change, but you *can* 'form' yourself the way you want. For example, wash your hands often during the day, to prevent the spread of infections. Cover your mouth when you sneeze, or cough. Once you get in the habit, these kinds of activities will become automatic, requiring no effort. You only can teach yourself to adhere to this routine.

What you are from birth is important, but it's more important what you make yourself become during life. You could not choose your birth, but you can choose who you become.

Education is the best investment. Stay in school as much as feasible. As for me, I have always been around schools of higher learning. I trained from 6 to 30 years of age, and still now I continue to learn. To study. To take courses. To read voraciously both professional books related to my work as well as non-fiction.

What you really own is what is in yourself. Improving yourself means more learning to be polite, to have nice manners, to never raise your voice, than buying a big house, a fancy car, or your own plane. These last things you can lose. You cannot lose an education.

Learn from your experiences. Wisdom can only be acquired by reflecting on your past actions, as well as those of others. To understand the road ahead, ask those that have already been along that road.

Look up to people you admire. Try to emulate whatever trait it is that you have a high regard for. You can make yourself a puzzle of all the best parts of others. There will always be individuals who are better than you at something, and others that are worse than you.

Do not compare yourself to the bad side of people, but to their strengths. If you miss a penalty at soccer, don't say: "Well, even Pele' missed a penalty shot once." Compare yourself to the best. Aim to have the qualities you admire in them. You will never find someone you want to be exactly like. But perhaps you'll want to emulate my optimism. Or mom's tidiness and organization, as well as our devotion to family.

Do not justify your shortcomings with the fact that they are not uncommon. Do not make the excuse that what you did wrong was done also by many others.

Find good 'wings' to follow. Mentors are wonderful. You make someone a mentor. If you find someone really good with computers, and that is what you want to learn, spend time with them. A stranger, seen only once, who is nice and lets an older person in the elevator and holds it for them, is a good example to follow.

Cherish more the acts than the words of mentors. See greatness more in their life, the movements, the actions, than in their speeches. Many can give great talks. But you should follow more those that 'walk the walk,' instead of those who 'talk the talk.'

By hanging around virtuous individuals, you become like them. Be aware, the same happens if you pass moments with vicious ones. By standing on the shoulders of giants, you'll see further, as was said by Isaac Newton.

You learn a lot from books, but often you discover even more from a tutor, a smart adviser. Once you find these kinds of people, keep them close and avail yourself of their input. Once you have absorbed the instruction, insert it in your own being, and adjust it to your own values, because in the end, you have to think with your own head.

Be around smart people. It is said that when an older person dies, it's like a whole library went up in flames. Learn from them, but do not believe everything they say. Often leaders such as presidents, ambassadors, CEOs, professors, deans, etc, have a lot to teach you.

Do not be afraid to approach them, and try to absorb their knowledge. If you discover that they are not so special after all, then you will have at least recognized that you are as smart and capable as anyone else.

Accept advice from the person who has expertise in the particular field. Or get experience by observing life carefully. You will need more than one mentor. The first guides are our parents. But I have learned and been inspired to be kinder from my father-in-law, to be more reliable from my wife, to write scientifically from Ron Wapner, to write personal non-medical non-fiction books from Ignazio Marino.

Experience will teach you to be kind. Respect your mentors, your teachers, your friends, and, really, everyone. Admiration is what they deserve. Esteem is often like love, reciprocal. Feeling your high opinion of them will often lead them to begin to show consideration for you, too.

Avoid boring people. Even James Watson, the discoverer of the structure of DNA, said so, not just me. Stay away from those who are full of themselves, who just like the sounds of their voice, and do not listen because they are not intelligent enough.

Be aware of what is wrong, and avoid it. Avoid bad friends. Avoid people without your values. At least be conscious of their limitations. For example, it is clear that Peppino, a high school classmate of mine, committed a felony when he did not pay hundreds of thousands of euros in taxes. He tried to hide this money in Switzerland, both for himself and for many others for whom he was the "accountant".

But it is as bad to hear from other friends justification for what he did. I heard from common buddies: "Oh, poor Peppino, they were too harsh on him." "Oh, it was not Euro 600,000, probably only 200,000." As though the lower amount would excuse him, and make him innocent.

In Italy, unfortunately, cheating, not paying taxes, is ok with vast segments of the population. The prime minister, Berlusconi, is the mirror of his country. Dishonesty is part of their lives. Do not make it part of yours. Honesty is one of the higher virtues. It makes you sleep well at night. Keep your dignity.

Be aware that people who profess to always know the truth are the ones who seldom know it. The best persons lack strong convictions, and are open to learn more. Keep an open mind, and do not be afraid to have opinions, but change them when new data becomes available. Base your opinions on facts. When you need to form an important opinion regarding some matter, try to go back and examine the original facts from the eye-witnesses.

<u>The glory of life is that there is always innovation</u>. Do not rely exclusively on traditions, but seek the best information from the most trusted sources. Be scientific about your thinking. Be passionately curious. Never passionately extremist. Seek the facts, not everyone's opinion. I believe in the wisdom of crowds, but even the majority's opinion can be wrong.

<u>Always look towards the future</u>. Seek opportunities and then follow them. Avoid getting used not to choose. Underachievers are too afraid of making choices that result in failure. Perfectionists are afraid of doing anything that will make them less acceptable or valued. Both types have decision paralysis, and won't reach their potential, and therefore their happiness.

<u>Celebrate successes</u>. But do not live on past achievements. Soon they'll be forgotten. So you must seek new ones.

You were given a <u>certain amount of 'talents'</u>. Make best use of them. Make sure they grow. Life is either a daring adventure using your talents at their best potential, or is a disappointment.

I always felt I was <u>given a tremendous amount of opportunities</u>. A good intelligent quotient, good education, economic stability and support from my parents, no major (or minor) life tragedies or stresses. Therefore, I've felt I needed to contribute more than others who did not have what I had. Suck all the marrow out of your life. Make your potential become reality.

<u>Be happy</u>. I have been born <u>optimistic</u>. It's a great gift. I think everyone was born happy. You already have happiness inside, like everyone else. If you do not feel happy, it might be it's because your illusions and negative feelings cloud your mind into sadness.

<u>Most problems are not with your spouse, your boss, your enemies</u>. They are with you, and how you approach them and life

in general. A positive attitude is contagious. A negative one, even more. A smile contaminates others with joy.

When it rains, I make myself like rain. I enjoy the peacefulness, the sound of the rain on the window. Or at least I think how much I'll enjoy the sun after the rain. Above the clouds, there is the sun. And it will not rain forever. I assure you. Do not be sad because it's raining.

Maintain your childish enthusiasm. There is a positive, carefree, innocent boy in each man; make sure he stays alive in you. Being serious is not by itself a sign of wisdom. In fact, I think that intelligence should make people learn by laughing.

Laughter is medicine. It's scientifically proven that laughing is good for you. Life is serious enough, and the mind deserves a break from the concentration to stay alive. The step from 'alive' to 'well' requires hilarity.

Travel. As you learn from different people, you learn from different places. Each place is a different page of the world book. It's hard to understand life if you only read a few pages of the book. You can skip a few pages, less interesting to you, but you should probably look at every major chapter.

You learn the most by teaching. That's when you are forced to acquire the facts, organize them, and come up with logic behind them. Your logic. First you need to know everything. Then you have to summarize it briefly. In a 10 minute speech, you can make 1 major point. In 30 minutes, at most 3 major points. As life is much more complex than that, you have the great challenge and responsibility to condense it to your own message. Later in your journey, once you have taught the facts, you will teach how to think and analyze properly.

The most important thing to teach is passion for solving problems so to benefit humankind. To awaken the joy of exerting one's qualities for high aims. A Chinese proverb says: "Give a man a fish, feed him for a day; teach him how to fish, feed him for a lifetime." That is how you should educate.

Only through teaching and research one realizes the holes in human knowledge. The less you know, the more you think you'll know. Many times I've envied, in a way, the ones who are ignorant. Ignorance can be bliss. But my mind has never allowed me to rest on ignorance.

Share your knowledge, your skill. It's a means to immortality, or at least enhances and prolongs your life. Happiness is when you make others happy. Happiness is a shared thing.

Be a finisher. Once I start writing a manuscript, or a book, I am going to see the whole project to its completion. I will not stop until it is in print and off my desk. In a way, until it is off my 'insides' and into the lives of others.

Find good hobbies. Sports, writing, travel, culture, theatre, music, and many others, are good ones. My biggest enemy in life has been boredom. Find leisurely pursuits that relax you, allowing yourself to be regenerated before you have to get back to your home and work duties.

Accept change. Too many individuals are stuck in the status-quo, and fear any minimal variation. The tomato comes from America, and it is now what Italians adore to have on their pizza and pasta. The potato also comes from South America, but Irish and Germans now could not live without it. In fact the Prussians were initially afraid of the change, but they eventually named the leader who diffused it in their land, the emperor Friedrich II, 'der Große', meaning 'the Great.' Change is often good, and the one who implements it gets praised.

What counts in life is what you earn yourself, with, as said in Italian, 'il sudore della fronte,' meaning 'the sweat of your forehead.' Building something yourself, gives satisfaction that is several times more fulfilling than anything you get without effort.

Do lead by example. The best authority is based on admiration. You do not have to lead. But, in small or big ways, you will at times find yourself at the helm of some project. Choose the position that allows you to sleep at night, not always the most popular. With power, comes responsibility. Let your team members participate. Listen to them, take their advice when it seems like they are right. Delegate some authority, let others lead parts of the project. Stay positive, and instill hope.

In November 2009, when you Andrea were only 11 (well, almost 12), I went to your parent-teacher conference. Your teacher Carla was all compliments. Except... she thought you were a <u>natural leader</u>, and should lead more. Apparently your classmates love to follow you (so Carla says), and you have to learn to lead them (so she says). This can be done by organizing them in team projects, speaking up at common meetings, etc.

If and once you lead, learn to <u>accept criticism</u>. Do not let it bother you. You can use criticism to improve. But a lot of criticism is just wrong, or contradictory. You cannot please everyone. The taller the tree, the more wind it gathers. The same with leadership. The more responsibility, the more people will feel entitled to judge you, and often to disapprove of you.

Grow a <u>thick skin to criticism</u>. Do not let it affect your positive attitude. The more successful you will be, the more enemies you will have. It is a fact of life. Even the most successful in life have a lot of opponents.

One of the secrets of success is to <u>be confident</u>. If you do not believe in yourself, others won't either. It's a vicious cycle. On the contrary, if you are self-assured, others will hold you in high esteem, and continue to foster your self-belief.

Another good way to improve is to <u>write down your ideas as you have them</u>. Often I get my best ideas in the morning, under the shower. Or while biking in the woods. It's important to have always around a piece of paper, or a little PDA or other collection device to store these ideas. Later, you can store them in an even better device (e.g. computer), and use them at the right time (e.g. a meeting, a project, a book, an article, a conversation, etc). Many of the ideas in this and my other books are a collection of these pieces of papers.

<u>I get ideas when I give my mind a break from deadlines at work</u>. Deadlines are great, and will get things done. But if you are

overwhelmed with work due for and to others, you never have time to develop yourself. Leonardo da Vinci said that genius is most active when doing the least work.

<u>Change into a better person every day</u>. Experiencing many situations, many friends, many countries, you can do that. And be sure you know who you are before changing, so your core values remain strong as your base.

<u>It's never too late to be what you might have been, what you want to become</u>. My mother always told me how young I was, how much more in front of me I had. One of my teachers of Orthopedics, a former Chair of the Department, got a Master in Public Health at 75. I admire people like him. I admire people who can switch career in their 40's, 50's', or even later. Especially those who do it as they have finally found their calling.

<u>Appreciate what you have</u>. Grass often only seems greener on the other side. So be simple. Do not get fixated on what you do not have. Enjoy what you already have. Often you fight for something, only to discover you did not need it that much. If beautiful things surround you all the time, you will get used to them. They will not seem beautiful anymore. Luxury is to be enjoyed seldom, so to appreciate it more.

<u>Do not accept risks that risk your health and life</u>. Smoking, excessive alcohol, illegal drugs, driving faster than 80 miles an hour, not wearing a helmet on a motorcycle, bungee-jumping, rock climbing without serious precautions, and similar activities, risk your life foolishly. Do not accept to exchange short-term thrills for permanent damage. You only have 1 life to live.

<u>Push yourself to make the future better than the past</u>. Each individual has a personal, moral obligation to make it so. Mahatma Gandhi said that you need 'to be the change you want to be.' I know this might be one of the most difficult teachings.

The school of life

Learning and teaching are to make you obey the truth. And the truth will make you happy and free.

School is a decent example of how life will be when you finish it. The ones who study better will be rewarded with the best grades. They will receive the admiration of both their bosses and their peers. They will be offered opportunities to get ahead of the others. They may be given rewards such as travel, money, better chances at other prizes, and, best of all, possibilities to face even more challenging tasks.

Sit in the first row in class. You will see better, hear better. It's easier to stay concentrated. You will remember more, and possibly then you will have to study less, as you have learned the lesson already while at school. The teacher will also notice you more, and that is, in general, good. Teachers notice who pays attention to them and who doesn't, and reward the alert pupils.

Do raise your hand when you know the answer to the question. Active participation is key in school and in life. Be enthusiastic. Share your knowledge. Let others know you are an asset to the team. You have a lot to contribute. You have the capacity to lead if called upon.

Be humble in school. You cannot raise your hand *every* time. Give also space to others, and also learn to listen. Finding a good balance between active participation and active listening is crucial. Never go to the extremes of blabbering constantly or resembling a mute statue.

Be courteous with your teachers. Sometimes you may know more than them. Do not make them feel degraded. During oral exams, if they contradict you in a controversial topic, do not raise your voice or make them feel stupid. If they are wrong, show them later the facts in a reverential manner.

Do your homework first, and play later. Duty first, recreation second. You will not have as much fun if part of your brain is thinking you still have work to do. Use your fresh energy to get your obligations done. You will complete your task better and faster. And playing later will be more serene and carefree.

I remember vividly when I was 8-10 years old and lived in my birthplace of Teramo, a small town in Italy. I would walk by myself back home from school. First I would eat heartily. Then I would do right away my less-than-an-hour of homework. I would be done at the latest by 2:30, or 3pm. Then I was free! I would run out and join my friends in the park or in the field along the river playing soccer. What liberty, independence, fun!

<u>Any subject is interesting if studied deeply</u>. Any topic is boring if only superficially conceptualized. Try to get to the inner core of the issues you are studying. Investigate the reasons why they happen. Moreover, aim to make yours the true and final meaning of the concept you are exploring.

<u>Prepare, prepare, prepare</u>. Once you know you will be tested, make sure you get ready to give your best, and nothing less. This can be for a written test, an oral exam, a paper, a lecture you need to give, an interview, just about anything. Once you do it for school, then it becomes a good habit.

My great friend and colleague Don Korkis said to me recently: "I remember when we walked out of the written obstetrics and gynecology national board exam at NYU in 1994 and you said, "I didn't think it would be so easy!"" I had forgotten this comment of mine. But I have not forgotten how much I studied before the exam and in general during the 4 years of residency, so to be ready to pass the test with ease.

The oral, 3-hour-long, one-examinee-versus-six-examiners obstetrics and gynecology national board exam is perhaps the most feared test for any physician in my field. In the elevators after the 3 hours, tightly squeezed among my peers who just finished like me the grueling ordeal, I sincerely and serenely stated: "Wow, that was fun." I felt that I had studied well, and so it was rewarding answering most questions. I received dozens of hateful looks. I am now one of only 32 national examiners for this test.

I was taught a lot of facts in schools. I spent hours memorizing notions. In a world of Wikipedia, Google, and the web in general, this is no longer absolutely necessary, even if it is still very important. What you need to learn is two basic things. First, where to find the facts, in particular the most accurate facts and data. Second, and even more important, you have to learn how to make best use of these facts.

There is a great difference from what you learn for general knowledge, and what you must use everyday for your occupation. Studying 8 years of ancient Latin and 5 of ancient Greek taught me most of all how to study (hard), as well as some of the general values narrated in the texts I translated to Italian. But I do not recall, or try even to remember all I memorized then.

Education is said to be what remains after you have forgotten the notions. Knowing the 'why' things happened is more important to know what happened. Napoleon invaded Russia in the early 1800s and, even if his soldiers got to Moscow, eventually lost the war by overextending his troops. Hitler repeated the exact same mistake in 1942-43.

World history repeats itself if leaders do not learn from previous mistakes. In fact a famous saying goes: "History does not repeat itself; it rhymes." The same will happen with you if you do not follow knowledge, and do not avoid ignorance, a major cause of evil. Educate yourself. Knowledge is power, safety, and happiness.

You should study best and know well the notions you need for work. That is why your years of school before college really serve the purpose to teach you how to study and to get you in the best and most appropriate school for you. The courses in university and (if you go) graduate school that pertain to what you will do in your job, which will pertain to a whopping 30-40 years of your life, will be most important. Keep those notes and books forever, get straight 'A's' in those classes.

Most importantly, continue to study all your life. In my profession, medicine, it is known that more than 50% of what we learn is obsolete and plain wrong just 20 years later. So, you have to keep on studying. You have to keep up-to-date. For most professions, this is paramount to keeping your job. In others like mine, it's essential to improve and save the lives of others.

Another major advantage to education is that <u>educated people live longer, happier lives</u>. This is scientifically proven. Better educated people establish healthier lifestyles, avoid health risk factors, have a better sense of self esteem and empowerment. They can cope with challenges and even adversities with better skill. No wonder they live happier, healthier lives!

<u>Read</u>. Get a list of the best books of all times, and read them. Read English, Spanish, French, German, Chinese, Japanese, Italian, Arabic, Hindu books, from all cultures. I love biographies, history books, books about our earth, or politics, religion, discoveries. Just read widely, and discover what you like best.

<u>Think like your best teachers</u>. Think like the people you admire. In general these are people who have studied, read, and traveled a lot to achieve a high grade of ability in dissecting facts. Behave so they love you and want to share their most valuable lessons.

<u>Live an evidence-based life</u>. Learn the facts before making a decision. In medicine, we call it 'evidence-based medicine.' Even in such an apparently precise science, physicians (who are just fallible men and women) tend to follow what makes sense. Often they make a decision based on a theory of their own, or which they have read. This is often wrong, and dangerous.

<u>Evidence-based medicine</u> is the concept of treating patients based on the best available evidence. The best available evidence usually comes from so-called 'randomized trials'. These are studies in which patients are assigned to a therapy or to another (or a placebo) based on the concept of the 'flip of a coin.' The 1,000 patients assigned by chance to antibiotic 'A' will be absolutely similar to the 1,000 patients assigned to antibiotic 'B'. The outcome will depend only on the efficacy of the antibiotics, since

all else (age, race, characteristics of the infection, other risk factors) will be equal in the two groups.

<u>Flossing your teeth is an example of living an evidence-based life</u>. So are: sleeping at least 8 hours a day on average; eating a 2,000 or less calories diet, with few saturated fats; exercising at least 2-3 times per week; avoiding constant stressful situations; wearing helmets while biking, seat belts while driving; avoiding smoking and illegal drugs; and thousands of other activities that have been tested with scientific studies and should now become part of your daily routine.

<u>Seek the truth</u>. Do not act based just on opinion or hearsay. There are data on just about anything in life. Do not jump to a conclusion without having reviewed carefully the information. This is not true just of science.

<u>Everything is really science</u>. My friend, physician and now Italian senator Ignazio Marino practices politics like he did liver transplantation. Deciding whether to amend a law on taxes requires studying carefully its history, and its consequences for the public, for the region, and for the state. How to kiss can be made scientific. How to walk. How to say hello. There is a science to everything.

Unfortunately, <u>often the experiences that make you grow the most are the painful ones</u>. Adversity reveals genius. If everything is well, you will not be pushed to your limits. <u>Competition will force you to improve yourself</u>, so seek it, do not shy from it. To be tested is good. Try the tough exam. Nietzsche, pushing this concept even further, said that 'what does not kill us makes us stronger.'

<u>Every problem is an opportunity in disguise</u>. In a crisis, exhibit your best character. Bill Clinton said that, 'the darker the night, the sweeter the victory.' And if the door shuts completely, a bigger door opens. Failure often brings wisdom. Do not be afraid of failure. If you are afraid of failure, then you are afraid of life.

Work hard

The secret of joy in work is contained in one word: excellence. To know how to do something well is to enjoy it.
  Pearl S. Buck

Try to choose a profession that you like so much that you do not notice that time passes. Einstein used to be so engrossed in his work that he would sometimes forget to eat lunch. As I write today, I stop at times to look at the clock on the computer. I think 5 minutes have passed, but the clock says 30 have passed. That tells me I'm having fun.

Look for a challenge. What is too easy won't test your mind. Aim high, for something that truly is a dream, and, with enough effort, you will get there. Do something that is mentally challenging, with smart people. Agree to be pushed to your limits. Albert Einstein taught that easily achieved goals are not the ones to pursue the most.

One should develop a wish to follow goals that can be achieved only through the greatest efforts. I never thought I could write a scientific article good enough for publication in one of the major medical journals. In fact, in 1996, when I did publish the first, a Jefferson resident made fun of me at the annual departmental party saying publicly that she did not think I had it in me.

I've published over 110 more of those. The challenge, including the fact that she did not think I could do it, pushed me to ask Informa Healthcare in 2005 to write a medical textbook. I've written and published 3 since, which have sold many thousands of copies worldwide, and were translated into several languages, including Turkish and Chinese.

These seemed like insurmountable tasks when I first started. In fact, many colleagues, even those who know me well, are still in awe of what I've done. But time, dedication, experience, have taught me that, to move a mountain, you must do it a stone at a time.

Too many, challenged with a task as big as moving a mountain, stop, look up at the mountain, and simply give up. I only look up once, then look down, and concentrate on dividing the task in small pieces, small enough so that I can achieve them. I say to myself: "This month, I'll move these 50 rocks."

So when, at the end of the month, the 50 rocks are moved, I'm satisfied. Never frustrated. And when, after a year, the mountain is moved, the reward of personal accomplishment is immense. In the meantime, during that year, I do not look at any other mountain.

I'm focused on the effort. I eat, I sleep, I love, and play with my kids, but my mind is soon wandering back to the mountain, and the next steps, on how to move it even more quickly, doing today tomorrow's assignment.

When you are learning to sail, do not be afraid of storms. Only challenges will improve you. A car is not made to stay in the garage. But most of its features are made to withstand rain, cold, heat, other difficult conditions, even crashes. Your body and soul also have to go through life being tested to improve.

There is always too much to do. If you are interested in life, the tasks will always be too many. But actually, that's the beauty of it. If you feel badly simply because there is more to do than you think you can do, you'll never be happy, but always annoyed. Be thankful for a life full of opportunities.

On the other hand, do not put too much on your plate. "I'll climb Mount Everest by next week" is not a good plan. But "I'll start training in the next 6 months to be fit enough for hiking above 8,000 meters" is a good start towards a tough goal.

I never thought I could run a marathon. I'm not a runner, but can certainly play soccer, tennis and many other aerobic sports for hours. Preparing for the marathon, my goal was to finish, not to break any particular time or record. I trained 3 months, running 10-20 miles a week. I did finish the New York City marathon in 2001.

A great personal accomplishment, of which I'm proud. Hard training, determination, and cheering from the millions of fans along the 26-mile route got me to my goal.

<u>Do something that is not good just for you, but also for the whole world</u>. If you strive for the environment, for justice, for rights of animals, for the health of others, or for their happiness, all is worthwhile. To check people at booths on the highway to get them to pay the tolls is not as rewarding as other activities.

<u>I enjoy being a doctor. I can see daily how I can improve the lives of patients and their loved ones</u>. Plus I get plenty of personal admiration, gratitude, and a nice check every two weeks. And I get challenged by new and difficult cases every week, if not daily. I have to still study and look things up. Even if I study incessantly, and write medical books and websites, as well as lecture frequently. I love this constant challenge. It keeps me young.

<u>One of the best things that can happen to you is the chance to work hard, very hard, for a worthwhile cause</u>. The word 'effort' precedes the word 'reward' even in the dictionary. 'No pain, no gain,' is an often true statement. I feel I've earned my day at work only when my butt begins to hurt after hours of sitting concentrated and productive at my desk. Remember, because it's hard, it does not mean it is not worth doing. Often the contrary is true. The easy is often not worthwhile, or at least not as rewarding.

<u>Add value to the earth during your stay</u>. Leave a mark, even if small. Stand for something bigger than yourself, as a leader or as a part of a great team. We are all looking for long lives, even for immortality. Use your life on some goal that will outlast it. Some effort for which you'll be remembered after you are gone. Or at least for some purpose that will benefit human beings.

<u>A life aimed at fulfilling personal desires, of no benefit to others, will eventually lead to disappointment</u>. You are still selfish when your happiness depends on the gain of others. All that we do is for our interest, everything. But you look much better to the community, and especially to yourself, when what you do not only benefits you (your self-esteem, pride, mind, etc), but also others.

So find something you really want to do, and then spend thousands of hours getting good. Some say that talent does not really exist. My godson, Adriano, is an excellent tennis player. His parents say he has talent. Truth is, Adriano has played 6-10 hours or more of tennis most weeks of the year since he was 5. It is repetition which makes greatness. That is how Roger Federer got to win the most slams of all players ever.

The best practice harder. Certainly their concentration, will to win, and many other abilities help, but thousands of hours of hard practice since they were very young is what made the Roger Federers, Tiger Woods, Michael Jordans, Joe DiMaggios of the world the best ever in their respective sports.

10,000 hours of practice, and you'll master it. Be it tennis, giving a lecture, learning a profession, giving hand shakes, etc. This is what Malcom Gladwell says makes 'outliers'. If you want to be good at something, do it all the time. Concentrate on the one time you feel you did it better than before, and implement that change, making it routine.

Drive and determination are the keys to achieving your success. Be dedicated, persistent. There are many men with talent, with lots of education, even geniuses, who end up unsuccessful. Persistence and determination alone are omnipotent, as said by President Coolidge and many others.

I have seen, for example in medical school, that there are people brighter than me. But, with a few more hours of studying, I could get the same, or often even better grades. Many leave work at 5pm. Staying in the quiet, productive work environment just 1 hour more, until 6pm, has been one of the secrets of my prolific medical writing, from which praise, recognition, fame, and promotions came.

Be grateful for your labor. Einstein said that 'work is the only thing that gives substance to life.' Your work will be what keeps steady the ship of your life. Make sure you can count on your profession, on your skills being appreciated and in demand.

<u>Feel good about your duty</u>. Embrace it. Make it fun, not bothersome. <u>Do more, see more, learn more, teach more</u>. See which ones of these you are best at, and enjoy it as much as you care to. Having a good time with your work is one of the requisites for joy.

<u>Do not get mad or surprised if you feel at times used by your company, or your boss</u>. If you are not productive, you will be out of your job. You must produce enough to pay your salary, your expenses, and often the salaries and expenses of many others, to ensure the viability of your institution. This is the nature of our world. But do not tolerate abuse.

<u>Don't put off until tomorrow what you could do today</u>. You'll be more serene not procrastinating. There is always something pressing on your mind. Without doing it, you'll lose concentration for doing anything else. So get the pressing difficult task done today!

<u>Do things well ahead of time</u>. If I have a new lecture to prepare, at least a month before I begin to search the whole literature on the topic. In Paris, in 2 weeks, I'll have to speak about a subject I have not spoken about before. At the French National Congress, with all the experts in the field there. I have read all their papers. I have already made the slides. Now I'll look at them every 3-5 days, rehearse in my head and aloud the speech, come up with a major opening to grab early everyone's attention.

<u>I work and work at it</u>, leaving nothing to chance, or at least as little as possible. The same with a new case, a surgical operation. I sleep well the night before exams, or before these major challenges, knowing that I'm well prepared. This gives me great calm, and confidence.

<u>Preparation</u> is a very important key to success. Use determination to get ready for whatever challenge is ahead of you. I do well now at lectures in front of hundreds of people because of intense training. I make sure I'm going to be the one who knows the most about the subject I'm lecturing on in the whole place.

Boredom may be your worst enemy. I never understood people who seek a day with nothing to do. To me, that's the worst that can happen to a man or a woman. Isolation and idleness often cause depression and an unhappy life. Leonardo da Vinci said that 'inaction saps the vigor of the mind.'

While you should follow these general principles, be tolerant with yourself. You'll have defeats you'll have to accept. Do not worry too much about being beaten. It's important to have the fortitude to get up. I'm always amazed, when I read the stories of accomplished men, how many times they were defeated in their early careers.

In 1956, John Fitzgerald Kennedy lost the Vice Presidential nomination at the Democratic convention to Senator Estes Kefauver of Tennessee. In 1980, Bill Clinton lost the Arkansas Gubernatorial election to Frank D. White. In 2000 Barack Obama lost the election for the US House of Representatives to Bobby Rush by a margin of 2-to-1. This list could go on for many pages. Do not, do not let defeats crush you.

I feel great after a day like today, where I have 'produced' something. I have created. I have helped. I'm going to enjoy playing sports or watching TV a lot more now. I feel like I've deserved it.

Study, continue to learn all your life, do something difficult that continuously stimulates your mind, continue to study even when you are old, never stop.

Diligence is what brings about good luck. To make a dream come true, the first requisite is the ability to dream; the second is persistence – a devotion to see the dream become reality. Genius is 1% inspiration, and 99% perspiration, as said by Thomas Edison.

Be a team player. Mix yourself with others. Do not be a loner. A perfect team is that made of 3-9 people, as I learned at Harvard's School of Public Health in 2002. Such a team beats the individual even if the individual is smart, accomplished, a 'Harvardian.' As my colleague Jason Baxter says, it's amazing what even just two persons can accomplish if they do not care who gets the credit.

The most famous football coach of all time, Vince Lombardi, said that what makes not just a team, but the whole of society work well, is <u>individual commitment to a group effort</u>. He was absolutely right, and his results show it. He won 5 football league championships with the Green Bay Packers in the early 1960's.

<u>Be on a good team</u>. James Watson, the one who, together with Francis Crick, discovered the structure of DNA, advises never to be the smartest in the room. I wonder: how did he avoid that? The point is to work with, and in general be around, people that are better than you at something, so you can learn from them and improve.

Be bothered by stupidity, with which you should not spend much time. But I'm even <u>more bothered by laziness</u>. On your team laziness should be less accepted than modest intelligence accompanied by commitment and hard work.

<u>Try to know what's going on above you</u>. Figure out what the boss of your boss is telling your boss. What are the priorities of the organization. If you can, have friends close to those who rule. You'll have a clear idea of what the future will bring, be them challenges or opportunities.

<u>Be on time</u>. Arrive at meetings, with your girlfriend, or your boss, or even your subordinates, 5 minutes early. This will be highly appreciated. Remember that first impressions count a lot, and the first impression is your punctuality. On time is the only right time.

<u>Perfection is the enemy of good</u>. Do things as well as you can, as they reflect on you to everyone else. But do not wait for perfect. You should aim for it, but be aware that perfection is hardly achievable on this planet. So be able to finish a product, even it is not perfect. Life is a flowing river, and you'll have a chance to continue to improve.

Remember that, as said by Woody Allen, <u>80% of success is showing up</u>. So participate. My roommate in medical school said that one cannot complain that he does not meet any girls if he studies in his room all the time, and never goes out. Make sure people are aware of you if you want to play a part.

Make sure you prioritize. Your services will be requested by many, for many tasks. Your curiosity may get you involved in too many projects. Learn to say 'no' to the ones you care less about, that are less fun for you. But do not say 'no' just because you may not be good enough.

Burnout comes when you put too much on your plate. Avoid stress. Even hard work should be rewarding in and of itself. Deadlines are good. Too many deadlines at the same time are bad. Let personal integrity guide you. Quality of life is a function of the choices you make.

One of the hardest decisions in my life was the one to accept or not the job of Director of Maternal-Fetal Medicine at Columbia University in 2004. I said 'no' because I would have had a commute of at least 30 minutes each way, and I would have been at work and away from my kids and wife many more hours. I had to give up a challenge I was looking for. I had to forget my pride in being called a 'Columbia Professor'. But it was probably a good choice.

Instead, when the same job had come available at Thomas Jefferson University in 2000, I jumped at the opportunity. In fact, I was not offered the job: I offered myself for it once it came available. I was young, inexperienced, but Dr. Bolognese saw in me potential, and promoted me to Director. It was the right move at the right time. My professional and personal life both continue to be of high quality.

Do not show off too much. Some people talk and talk, at meetings, in regular conversation. They have nothing new or interesting to say, but they feel that saying something will make them look better. Quite the contrary. People get points on my score sheet only if what they say is intelligent and adds to solving the problem. Otherwise, they risk loosing points. I think I got to be a leader by speaking parsimoniously, but making it count when I do.

In the end, <u>make also sure not to let work take over your life</u>. I like my work, but I love my wife. Make sure your priorities are right. Once my nephew got in a life-threatening car accident, I quit work for 4 days and flew to him to make sure he was ok.

<u>There is no limit to what you can achieve through dedication. Be patient, sets your goals high, and keep focused on them. Success is getting up in the morning and being excited about what you do, and flying out the door. Happy.</u>

Play hard

*It's not important what you find at the end of your run;
What counts is what you feel during it.*
Movie "The night before the exams"

<u>I know I have always played hard</u>, as well as worked hard. I have played soccer, tennis, basketball, swimming, and many other sports all my life, even now in my 40's. When I work, and when I play, I respect the rules. I'm honest. Not smoking or doing drugs, eating healthy, exercising, come naturally when you have these goals. I know a tenured professor is not supposed to sweat like a horse playing soccer. But I love playing soccer, this is who I am.

<u>When I judge myself</u>, I know that I work a lot, but I also know that I play more than most other people. This is where I found my balance. I do not want life to slip by me, but I want to be as active as possible, and make a difference.

<u>Find yourself a good hobby</u>. When I play soccer, I forget about the taxes to pay, the difficulty at work, the small family issues. My mind is free, in fact empty of everything; my focus is on the ball, on helping my friends, and on scoring. I feel bliss.

<u>The endorphins I gain after exercise improve my mood</u>. I feel elated. At 5pm, I'm usually tired and unable to concentrate on patients' issues or writing any more manuscripts. I can barely get enough energy to get up from my desk chair. I often think of steering my bike away from the gym and straight home.

At 5:30pm, during <u>swimming</u>, I feel my mind wander, my body finding rhythm, the splashes of the clear water soothing music to my ears. Just 20 minutes, 36-40 laps. Then a nice shower. Walking out of the gym, I feel like another person. Biking home I sing in happiness, my mood restored, in fact as good as it was that early morning. And life looks wonderful to my soul.

Brisk walking, especially after a large meal or after dinner, a light jog, the treadmill while you watch TV: <u>exercise does not have to be harsh</u>. In fact contact sports are to be avoided if you want to stay clear of injuries. 30 minutes per work-out, or at least breaking a sweat, done most days of your life, will make you happy. Forget about living longer: we are talking happiness! And happiness means success.

Organizing my coin or stamp collection, making a model plane, reading a good book, occasionally riding a friend's motorcycle all give me similar feelings of peace, tranquility. Watching soccer on TV may be useless, but certainly helps me relax. Find out what gives you serenity, and do it.

People should not stop playing just because they grow old. In fact, I believe people grow old because they stop playing. You can be in the best shape and mood of your life when you are 60 or 70. In fact, it is scientifically proven that the older you get, the more exercise your aging muscles and bones need.

Girls

Girls are like motorcycles: all beautiful.
Marco Carrara

There over 7 billion people in the world, more than half females. If you take into account ages 20-40, <u>you can choose from over one BILLION girls</u>. Do not keep numbers, but make sure you meet and get to know well many different types of girls, before settling with one for the rest of your life.

<u>Initially go out with many girls, so you can understand which kind is for you.</u> It is difficult to know if a girl is the right one for you if she is the only one you ever knew. I am in general against revivals, or going out with a girl you broke up with before. But, even if you happen to find the 'perfect' girl before 25-30 years old, it might be best to see others to make sure 'she is the one'.

<u>It's risky to marry in your early 20's</u>, after having gone out with only a handful of girls. Often the young spouse will be wondering later in life about other possibilities. If one has dated long and wide in the formative stages of life, there will be fewer regrets in adulthood. Most importantly, an adequate dating period demonstrates that there is no absolute perfect match, so that one is more able to stay happy with the mate finally picked for life.

<u>For me, even if I had met my 'missing rib' when I was 25, I would not have been able to marry her and spend my whole life happily with her.</u> I was still unsure what person I really was. And consequently I did not know what person was best for me (and what kind of me was best for her).

<u>I'm not talking about blond vs brunette</u>. And even this changed (blond before 20, brunette after). Tall or short? Athletic or feminine? College-educated or street-smart? Tough-minded or submissive? International or local girl? So many choices, so many traits. Only by experiencing the different types you think might make a good match with you, can you decide wisely.

<u>Have fun, but always respect women</u>. They do not deserve being cheated on if you are in a serious relationship. Some of your rapports won't be serious, but the ones that are should be properly managed. It's difficult enough to make one girl happy, almost impossible to make more than one truly happy at the same time.

<u>Do not lose hope if the one you think is the right one 'declines' you</u>. A better one is probably around the corner. But if you really like a girl, do not give up the first time she says 'no'. Persistence pays. Find out what she likes. If you can change yourself a bit so to satisfy her likings, then do it. But you cannot become a completely different person to please someone. You'd become miserable in long term. Do not waste time with someone who does not love *you*, but love instead some other idea they want you to fit into.

<u>Remember that girls like boys, at least as much as we like them</u>. They can make us very happy, but so can we make them happy. We depend on women just as they depend on us. Respect them, and expect the same back. Love them, and expect reciprocity. We are a bit more romantic, they are a bit more realistic.

<u>Do not settle too easily</u>. There are probably many women who are right for you. So leave to another guy the one who is not right for you. And let people, especially your family and closest friends, give you some advice. It is usually wise. In the end, though, you choose, and you bear the consequences.

Life-long partner

Happy wife, happy life.

<u>Choose your 'significant other for life', i.e. your wife, very wisely</u>. I even wrote an 'identikit' of the woman I wanted. I suggest you do the same. Make sure the woman you marry is somewhat similar to what you have dreamed for yourself. Too often you are struck by the external looks. Make sure the character traits you are looking for are also there.

<u>The key to intelligent children is to marry an intelligent wife</u>. It is a gift to live with someone, your partner, who is wiser than you. Often the right person solves many problems in your life. She puts your head back on your shoulders. Make sure your wife is intelligent above all other qualities.

<u>You will have differences with her</u>. Louis Armstrong said "You say tomato, I say tomato", pronouncing slightly differently the first 'a', with a hard 'a', than the second, with a soft 'a'. This minor difference made him say also, and title this song, 'Let's call the whole thing off'. And this is indeed a trivial divergence.

<u>You can overcome these differences only by open communication with a smart partner</u>. After civil discussion, you two may still disagree, but a bright person will at least understand and 'see' your point, respecting it and you. And, with time, several differences will be diminished by this clever dialogue.

<u>Your partner is your co-pilot</u>. If you are missing, she can take over. You must be able to have complete trust in her. You must know her well, as she must know you, too. This means your strengths, your weaknesses. All your abilities, values. Any activity done by two people is done more safely and effectively than by just one.

<u>Your co-pilot must have a similar level of skills to yours</u>. I always found it difficult for an astrophysicist and a maid to really be happy together. It can happen if the maid is not only bright but has also studied in college or even past it, and is interested in

continuing to learn. But the secretary marrying the expert professional with many more years of schooling may never be able to really comprehend and satisfy the whole spirit of the partner. Very sad, but at times painfully true.

Our companion should be able to understand our discourse about work matters. Our professional life is important, and the relationship is more accomplished if all our thoughts and preoccupations can be shared. There is nothing worse in a rapport than feeling lonely with someone right next to you. It's hard to share neurosurgery concerns with someone who has barely finished high school.

The person you want to marry is someone who makes you better. Often I think that some of my best characteristics I owe to Paola. She makes me faithful. She makes me better organized. She makes me more reliable. She makes me happy. She makes me enviable. She is indeed smarter than me, and there is nothing she cannot give me good advice on.

Often I think that Paola makes me feel more that I think I am. She told me, 'I love you because you are 'in gamba'. This is an untranslatable Italian expression, which vaguely means 'wise and clever.' She told me, 'Tomorrow is a sad day because I won't see you.' She told me these two things only once each. But it counted. It mattered more than if she told them to me a thousand times. This is how she loves me. Ain't I a lucky guy?

Finding your life-long significant other is indeed the most important decision you will ever make. You will spend hopefully more than 40, maybe 50 years with her. More than with anybody else. She will for sure change your life, in many ways. I wish for you to be as lucky finding your companion as I was encountering your mother.

Do not make quick decisions regarding who you'll spend the rest of your life with. Falling in love does not mean they are a good fit for you. I've fallen in love to protect someone. To find companionship. Because I needed to. True love though requires lots of time. You need to understand each other, test each other in many situations, both happy and difficult.

You cannot choose a girl in the darkness of a night club, and right away pretend to know you'll be happy with her, every day of the rest of your life. Know her intimately, understand what she values, what she wants in life and in you. Understand where she comes from, her culture, her family.

You often will fall in love not with the person herself, but with the idea you have of her. You hope so much you have found the right person, that you create one to fit your previously developed ideal. I have done this many times, it's easy and even fun to do. But it does not work.

You cannot change people much. If the girl you are dating is a pessimist, either you accept her like that, and even love her when she manifests this side of her character, or you move on and find someone without this trait, which you cannot tolerate and live with.

It's easy sometimes to fall in love with the weak. To fall in love with those who need it most. I once feel in love and had a 2-year relationship with someone who had attempted suicide a year before we met. In general, helping the needy is one of the best acts one can ever do. In this case, her depression made me depressed, and I was often unable to help her, falling into pessimism with her. Clearly we would not have been happy together.

Most people have to first meet many who are not right for them. This is the only way to slowly realize who would be right for you. I came up with a list of traits of my ideal girl when I was in my 20's and dating. Paola fits most of the qualifications, but I did not marry just because of that.

I married her because she is sharp, she is caring, because she loves me with facts and not with words, because she understands me and values me, because she has my same core values of honesty, hard work, and family. The small differences are easily worked out when the basis is strong.

Happy wife, happy life. This is a phrase I coined to emphasize how your wife will be the most important person in your life to achieve joy. You cannot be happy at work, playing sports, chatting with your friends, unless you have a positive bond with your significant other.

Your partner is the one with whom you share the duties of the present and with whom you plan the future. You divide with her the house and family chores. She is your 'number 1' advisor. You want a strong, brilliant counselor. A consultant devoted to your common goals.

A mistake is to expect too much from your partner. Remember that nobody is perfect. Your wife cannot be everything for you. You also need friends to play soccer with, mentors at work, advisors for taxes, editors to correct your books, etc. One person cannot be everything, cannot fulfill all of our needs.

When you disagree with the ones you love, do not scream. Do not call them names you'll later regret. Do not use vulgar words as the 'f' word. Do not bring back old arguments. Be able to concentrate on the current events. Love is the ability to reconcile your differences. With friendship, it is usually enough to manage and foster your similarities. With love, you need to do both. Tolerate each other with affection.

Often you miss what you do not have. A prostitute misses God. A priest may miss sex. Once you are married, you'll miss dating. When you date, sometimes you'll envy the ones who are happily married. Do not let this bother you. Make your choices wisely. Date a lot when you are young, to get it out of your system.

One of the great miracles of love is that you learn to love the imperfections in your partner. In 'Good Will Hunting', Robin Williams mourns for the loss of his wife while talking with Matt Damon. Matt asks him what he most misses about his wife. "She used to fart in bed, and pull the covers over my head", says Robin Williams. That is great. The husband misses her farts!

Yes, after years of happy living together, even crooked teeth or bad habits are aspects you learn to love. That is what love is about. Forgiving the imperfections of the other. Knowing that a bad hair day does not take away from so many core virtues.

My wife may love me more than I love her, because she shows it to me not with words, but with facts. Love is not just repeating 'I love you'. Love is caring for the other so as to give them unexpected presents of exactly what they want. Love is behaving to please them. Is seeing the movie or show you do not like but they adore. Doing laundry, cleaning the table, doing the dishes, so the other does not have to. As Ben Franklin said, "In life, well done is better than well said."

True, everlasting love grows slowly like a pearl in an oyster. It feeds on open communication. On trust. On respect. On mutual help. The roles of each partner get defined better and better with time. Each must strive to better understand the other by listening with both mind and soul, and changing to best fit the partner. This takes decades, but brings great rewards if done correctly. It's patient work.

The fact that someone does not love you the way you expect them to, does not mean they do not love you to their fullest. We are all different. While we all share >99.9% of identical DNA, that 0.1% of difference, plus the different cultural habits we have acquired before meeting each other, are what can keep us apart.

Some display love by hugging, some by baking a cake, some by holding your hand, some by giving a thoughtful gift. We are all somewhat different, and we should accept this truth. I doubt you won't be happy because your companion does not 'love you enough' to come out and dance with you. They might not reveal their love in a physical manner, but more by words, or acts, or by writing a book.

Give love and kindness, without necessarily demanding anything in return, at least not right away. We expect too much from others at times. Giving is better than receiving. Before demanding a favor, let's first donate a kind act ourselves.

Be on your wife's side, not on your mother's. Your wife is more important than your mother. Your family is me, mom, and your brother for now. But, once you get married, your family becomes your wife. Dedicate yourself to her and any kids you might be fortunate enough to have.

<u>Monogamy</u>. I'm still unsure we humans were made to be partners with only one person for so many years. But our society and current values certainly demand it. I highly recommend it, obviously from both partners. Respect and trust, are the 'sine-qua-non' of a successful loving partnership.

Family

What you give is yours forever;
What you keep is lost forever.

Create for yourself a new family, your family, and love them madly. Family is one of the best things you can ever donate to yourself and the world. A significant other whom you love is the first step. Then, hopefully, helping together a bunch of kids to grow up is a miracle of joy impossible to describe to those not fortunate enough to have had them.

Being surrounded by love at home should be the base for your life. It's not optional. It's a must. Without this base, it's difficult to find true happiness. You can see there are many people out there singing of their joy in marriage, and fatherhood / motherhood. It is hard to be happy in our society without good companionship.

Give, so that people will love you. Give to the people you want to receive from. And to the people with whom you'll have to interact often and for a long time: best examples are your family members. You also should be nice at work, but your family should be first, before work.

Home is where your family is. It does not matter if you live in Peking or Nairobi. It's important you are next to your wife and kids. The warmth, the feelings of affections they'll provide you, are needed to live. Do not go more than a week or two without seeing them, if you can.

Foster family relationships in detail. Behave in a way that makes them better. Be a good example. Spend quality time with them. Care for their preferences. Call your dear ones who live far away often on the phone, or email them, poke them on facebook, see them and talk to them via skype. Stay in constant contact, share your lives.

Children

What the dictionary says about dad: a dad is one who loves you and cares for you and you love him back.
Pietro Berghella (my son, then 9 years old)

July 8th, 1997
Dear Andrea,
when you'll read these phrases of mine you'll laugh, because possibly in your times mind-writing will be a reality. We know now you have 46 chromosomes, the last pair is XY. You also have my translocation from Y to 15, and (we hope) viceversa. By good fortune, you are Kell negative.

Parents worry for their kids since they are young. So many things can go wrong. My translocation could have been imbalanced, and cause you death, or disease. If you were Kell positive, as mom Paola is Kell negative, she would have developed antibodies that could have harmed your future brothers or sisters.

I'm suffering a bit, nervous. Friday the 11th you'll be 20 weeks. You'll get an anatomy ultrasound, to make sure all your organs are fine. You have passed all the tests so far with a perfect score. You'll have to take so many more tests in your life. I hope the trend continues.

You have already visited Beverly Hills, a suburb of Los Angeles. In 2 weeks you'll take your first trip to Italy. Aren't you happy? One day, I can imagine it now, you'll tell me if you want to live here in the US or in Italy. Or perhaps Peking? Who knows…
Ciao.
Papa' (!!!!!)

Your kids will be one of the best things that will ever happen to you. It is hard to explain the feeling to those who never had children. Kids are a piece of your heart. If you get this great gift of life, kiss them, hug them, all the time. Tell them you love them a lot.

Love makes people strong. I could go out and conquer my world because I was sure of my parent's passion for me. I knew I would always have a shelter, financial security, and adoration no matter what. This gave me the power to test myself, without fear of failing. My confidence was based on my mother saying I was 'the best.'

Apart from love, the other critical thing to give your children is your time. We parents are the examples they will follow. The providers of the advice they most seek. Being physically near them is what they deserve. You cannot walk away after providing the gamete.

Provide your kids with guidance. Be a good example they can follow. Show them other fine models of humanity. You are the main instructor, but cannot do this alone. Support them along the way, by checking their progress. Provide positive reinforcement for good behavior, advice to avoid bad behavior. Check their progress every step, check their homework, talk with their teachers, their friends.

Remember that your kids will treat others as others have treated them. The principal others are you and your wife, so make sure you provide a good example. Behave as you would want your kids to behave, and they will follow. The best teaching is by example. Anthony De Mello has written interesting books about this concept.

It is very difficult to properly educate kids. It's a tremendous responsibility. In this situation of parent-child, you deeply influence a life. I have tried to praise you not just when you won. It is easy to say 'congratulations on your victory' after one of your soccer matches. It is more complicated to make you see your shortcomings, but also your worth, in defeat.

<u>Chess was a good example</u>. Pietro won a match in 4 moves in his first ever National tournament in Nashville, in first grade. My congratulations were much bigger in his second match, when he beat the daughter of the coach of the Texas team, after 2 hours of 'braining' over the chessboard.

The first victory was due to a trick Pietro learned from his coach. My teaching was that the second game was going to be much harder. The second victory came from his very young neurons, a win of concentration and determination.

He then lost the third game, but again played his best, as his coach told me. <u>I instructed him to place the focus on the effort</u>: sometimes the best effort results in second place, or even a loss, but should nonetheless be praised. He got much more praise for this loss than for the first easy win over a weak adversary.

<u>Congratulate children for the actions</u> that led to their good grades and their trophies. Do not praise the trophy in itself, but the hard work that led to the win. "You must be proud of yourself," tell him/her. Make him/her focus and reflect on how his/her application to improve led to a better result. <u>They need to understand deeply the connection between effort and outcome</u>.

<u>It's very difficult to be a parent, as well as being a son</u>. Feelings and emotions, as well as love in general, are hard to interpret at times. In the world everything is relative. For example, I might get an A on all my exams. Instead a sibling, or another family member, usually gets barely a D, the minimum. At times, he or she fails.

Well, <u>a parent will often congratulate more the bad student/son for the D then the more hard-working student/son when he gets the usual A</u>. Is that fair? I think so. Sometimes a parent needs to support more the weaker, more feeble, maybe even needier son or daughter.

<u>Sometimes a parent needs also to be closer to the kid who complains more, who demands more attention</u>. Not necessarily because they deserve it, but because they need it more. And this a parent understands well. So, if you are a failure, your mother might

love you more than your brother or sister who is a great success. Your parents might feel they did something wrong, and are the cause of your defeats. Either because they passed the wrong genetic material, or they did not educate you well enough. This is the way of parenthood.

<u>Parents are not givers of jobs</u>. You should secure one good one by yourself. Parents are not bank tellers. I was a waiter and a librarian in college, and those few dollars earned made me proud. Count on me and mommy until you have to, but, once you are done with your studies, you'll see how wonderful it is to receive a check with your name on it.

Moreover, <u>parents are not means to an inheritance</u>. I have seen people wait their whole life for money from an inheritance. For an apartment, a villa, some jewel. You should use your inheritance as money in the bank, not to be touched. The thought that one day you might be given some funds from your parents should provide only reassurance. So that if one day you hit a difficult moment, by losing your job or not being able for whatever other reason to provide for yourself or your family, some other means of buying food and providing shelter is available to you.

<u>But you will feel proudest if you earn yourself all you and your family need</u>, so that, when and if you get the inheritance, you can use it for a trip around the world and to assure your kids the same chances and support you have had.

<u>Do not spoil your children</u>. Allowing every wish to be fulfilled, and every demand to be met, does not mean you love them. We parents want to give the best to our kids. The other day Pietro asked for a handkerchief. I kept the dirty old one for myself, and gave him a clean and soft one. Make sure they feel you love them. But also that rewards demand their labor. If they do their homework before playing, they can then get, occasionally, a new toy. They should understand when they are very young that effort leads to recompense, and idleness to despair.

<u>Give them the chance to prove themselves</u>, without overburdening them with your presence, your successes. Make

sure they have opportunities in life. Make sure you do not force your career onto them. They already compare themselves a lot to you; do not make them feel 'second'. They do not have to copy you, or beat you, to succeed. A Chinese proverb says, "Do not forget that they are your progeny, but you do not own them."

<u>You are lucky, as you have a sibling</u>. A brother who adores you. A brother on whom you can rely the rest of your life. Before Pietro was born, Andrea would hug him, by spreading his arms across Paola's belly. Before Pietro could walk, he was already looking up in adoration to Andrea, his hero.

<u>Never fight</u>. You love each other too much. Andrea used to give the feeding-bottle full of milk to the voracious Pietro when Pietro was 6 months and Andrea only 2 years old. Andrea ran to Pietro when he cried trying to console him. Pietro's great satisfaction in life is to make Andrea laugh.

<u>You love each other to the highest possible degree</u>. Maybe because you were born both in the 'city of brotherly love,' Philadelphia. I do not recall ever fighting with my brother Michele. There is a fraternal bond that is unbreakable. Do not let anyone in between.

<u>You are a team</u>. Do as much as you need to as a team. You'd be able to sound off each other many big decisions in life. Teams do better than individuals. Family is one of the best teams, since they won't betray you, and are on your side.

<u>Make sure to improve your behavior compared to us, your own parents</u>. Learn from our shortcomings. I felt my father was away a little too much when we were young, as many fathers of his generation. I have pushed myself to be more present in your daily life. To be an example not just by being absent and showing a hard work ethic.

<u>Perhaps you think I joke around a bit too much</u>. That I have written too much. That I could not keep secrets well. Whatever it is, improve on what I have done. Copy what you think was just and a good example.

On a selfish note, passing on your best teachings to your kids and, in general, to the next generation, makes you live forever. Because from our tree, these new leaves have some of ourselves in them, and will continue life forever. When I salute with my favorite toast, which is 'To the next generation,' I salute their and my future. So long as you or your teachings are remembered, you won't die.

In the end, as long as your kids do well, and make you proud, that's all that really matters.

Friends

Finding a friend is finding a treasure.
Italian proverb

Friends are people we can trust. Persons we can tell everything to. You do not expect them to cheat on you, to let you down. They should be loyal to you, helping especially in the challenging times of your life.

Friends are people you want to share your joys with. The ones you can tell your successes to without feeling immodest. Even more importantly, they are the ones that you can lean on when you are down and feel defeated.

Approach others as potential friends. Be optimistic initially regarding their intentions, their qualities, their projects. Life is full of heroes, of virtuous, honest people. But be careful to quickly identify the ones who are vicious, untrustworthy, dangerous. Once you have identified the malicious ones, stay clear of them.

True friends are hard to find. An Arab proverb says, "All the camels in the desert are not sufficient enough to buy a friend." You will meet thousands of people, but only some have the right qualities and attributes. Just as you should identify the traits you want in a significant other, list the characteristics of people you want to be friends with. For me, these traits are numerous.

Honesty is perhaps the most important one. The next one is sincerity, in terms of being able to share the innermost problems, the most intimate thoughts, the secrets. Secrets should not exist between true friends. A friend should have time to dedicate to you, and be easily available. Being a friend requires accessibility, and commitment to be on hand when needed.

Find friends who are intelligent, who make you better. Do not try to befriend people just because they are famous, or because others want to be with them, as they are 'fashionable'. Do not judge people based on external appearances, such as clothes, money, car, house. But evaluate their values, their determination to worthy causes, their selflessness, seriousness, authenticity.

<u>Cherish your friends</u>. Once you have found someone you can trust and lean on, keep in touch. Go out with them. Talk to them often. Make sure they trust you as well, and that the trust is mutual. Having a friend is a bit like having a lover. They need to be cultivated. But they should be more forgiving.

<u>Friends are best enjoyed one-on-one</u>. Just like a lover. There is as much jealousy in friendship as there is in a love relationship. It can be hard to divide your time fairly when among a few true friends. Each wants your attention. It's fun to be with a few of them, but make sure they each feel your companionship. The most intimate considerations are hard to share unless you have your hand on their shoulder and you are looking caringly in their eyes.

<u>Send best wishes to your friends on their birthdays.</u> Each of us is a bit romantic about their birthday. As we get to be 'less young', birthdays are not as carefree, but acquire a tint of sadness, as they remind us we are closer to the end. So people like to be remembered on their big day; it makes them feel loved.

<u>Be generous in gifts for others</u>. They do not need to be expensive. But they should be thoughtful. It's best to buy anniversary gifts during the year, when you find the object that will make that person happy, that she desires. Not the day before the event. In fact, it's better to come empty-handed to a birthday party, but give a thoughtful gift at another time, unexpected. The birthday gift can receive little attention lost among all the others. Your unexpected gift will be unique, and shine in its solitude.

<u>Go to weddings, and even more to funerals</u>. Call and visit people sick in the hospital. Check how they are doing. These are the moments they remember more. These are the moments a friend should be a friend. Your buddy will be forever thankful.

<u>Be careful which friends you hang around with</u>. Spend time with the ones who are truthful, the ones who have your same values. Spend time with those who love you. Keep close with those you hold in high esteem, even if they live far.

<u>At the end of life, you'll have only 10 or so people you really have cared a lot for</u>. Most are family, some are friends. Identify who these are early on, fostering the relationship, so you do not regret having lost their trust and intimacy later in life.

The family you were born into, you cannot choose. But <u>you can choose your friends</u>. Make sure you hang around the ones you hold in high esteem. The ones you have confidence in. The ones you want and will follow advice from.

Communicate

A teacher affects eternity;
He can never tell when his influence stops.
                              Henry Adams

It's essential to communicate with others. To converse with them. Study and learn your fellow creature. Be interested in others. You can learn from any single human. Everybody can pass along an experience, a piece of evidence you do not know yet. This will enrich you.

People are not mind-readers, so make sure you share your ideas with them, too. This is important, with your significant other, your children, your friends. But also with everyone else you come in significant contact with. Learn to communicate well, and you'll have a happier life.

It's important to pay attention to what you say. Choose your words carefully. Do not rush into a conversation before having organized in your head what you are going to say.

It does not take much to say the truth. Long speeches are those that are most empty. Incompetence is often linked to an excessive use of words. Be direct. Be concise. Be candid. Be accurate.

It's even more important to focus on 'how' you say it. Your tone of voice is often more telling than the statement you make. Be passionate when needed. Be diplomatic most times. Always be respectful, avoiding offending anyone, ever. Speak when you are angry and you will make the best speech you will ever regret.

Shake hands well. With your full hand. And looking the person straight in their eyes. Make him or her feel they have your complete attention. First impressions last forever. A few seconds of your full one-on-one consideration are worth a lot more than thousands of distracted encounters.

Communicating allows you to form a team, as you can then have more people deliver your message or agree with you. The absence of my father so often at work away from family could have been perceived as negative. Instead, my mother, a great co-pilot for my father, continually praised him, so that he became for us an idol for sacrifice and hard work.

Be even-tempered. Deliver your message calmly, but with confidence. Elaborate it so it is clear, short and to the point, easy to remember. So that people become aware of your acumen, of your erudition, of your wisdom. And of your excellent manners.

In communication, it's important to give, not only to receive. Whatever you do, teach your skills to young people. This is like seeding a field. It will take time to see the results of your efforts. But years later, it's wonderful to see the seeds germinating. Your impact on the world will be much bigger than if you keep what you know all for yourself.

What you keep will die, what you give away will live forever. Share what you know, do not enter your tomb with any information unrevealed. You can share by speech, via conversations, lectures, meetings, conferences. I have also learned to share with the printed word. Articles, books, notes, poetry. We humans have a lot of common events and emotions we all go through, and it's wonderful to convey to others our experience.

Educating will keep you in close contact with children and young adults, who are the future of the world. They have the new ideas, the passion, the will to improve what's around them. Their contact will keep you young.

Rare persons are indeed devilish. Stay away from them. Criminals exist. But do not accuse excessively. Once I got upset on a plane from Munich to Philadelphia, when the German man seated behind me asked me to raise my seat, in front of him. I showed him my seat was smaller than his. My emergency-exit seat had actually no leg room; his did. I also showed him I'm at least 4-5 inches taller than him.

I thought he was evil to expect *me* to do him a favor. Some people can see only their own good. They seem not to care about the well-being of others. Do not see harm unless it is towards them.

But, in general, I have had the sensation that most people are nice. Even if they might not always appear so. He probably did not mean wickedness.

There is nothing more sterile and useless than vengeance. Never, ever retaliate. If you do not trust someone, if you feel they have been unjust and mean towards you, just avoid them. Revenge against them reinforces their behavior, makes them stronger, gives them a chance for more evil acts, and diminishes you to their unworthy level. You have nothing to gain from vengeance.

We often hate what we do not know. The unknown scares us. In general, the more I study a fact, the more interested I become. The majority of times, it is the same with people. The more we share with someone, the more we discover their good traits, our commonalities. Do not judge negatively too quickly. Trust but verify.

Keep in shape

Mens sana in corpore sano. [Healthy mind in healthy body]
Ancient Roman saying

John F. Kennedy said it well: "The Greeks understood that mind and body must develop in harmonious proportion to produce a creative intelligence." And so did the most brilliant intelligence of our earliest days - Thomas Jefferson - when he said that not less than two hours a day should be devoted to exercise. If the man who wrote the Declaration of Independence, was Secretary of State, and twice President could give it two hours, we should give it at least 20 minutes.

Even the Romans had a wonderful maxim about exercise: "Mens sana in corpore sano." A sound mind should reside in a sound body. The two depend on each other. Concentrate for example on how you feel after exercise.

I get a high of energy and good will after I exercise. At 5pm, after a day full of decisions to make and deadlines to beat, I feel exhausted, empty, tired, useless. I need great willpower to go to the gym and not home to veg in front of the TV. Even taking off my socks in the locker-room seems too much of an activity for me. But let me describe to you once again what happens once I start exercising.

I jump in the clear water of the swimming pool. I'm still afraid I might drown from lack of force. But I push myself. I dive in, and take the first stroke in free style. The water is a bit cold. So I take another stroke, and then another. By the forth or fifth stroke, I'm already in sync. "I can do this!" I shout to my brain, elated.

My body goes into auto-pilot. I forget all the work my reborn muscles are doing to transport my 210 pounds from one end of the pool to the other. My body is back in its first element. The spent batteries recharge, by themselves, just being allowed to do what they are designed to do.

With my body, so goes my soul. The brain is not a muscle. But the feeling of wellness gained by my muscle fibers, by my bones, by my physical body, gets transmitted unconsciously to my head. My mind wanders, like in a dream-like state. I do not control it any more either. It's by itself, unleashed. This is its way of regenerating. Both mind and body absorb the new oxygen. Free radicals and any inflammation get wiped out. I *feel* the endorphins curing me.

My improved mood makes me more efficient. After exercise, it's like I have just woken up. I'm fresh. I can take on a task I was afraid of just an hour earlier. I'm hopping while walking down the street back home. I'm singing cheerfully.

The same evening, as well as the next day, the sore muscles remind me of the recent pleasures of exercise. The tired body continues to provide energy to the mind. I am proud of what I have done the day before. The endorphins are still floating in my body and soul. Being physically tired benefits my mind.

Many of us take their car to the shop routinely, and keep on cleaning it, changing the oil religiously. Most keep their house clean, fix any leak, dust and shine every corner. We need to dust and shine our body, too. Proper eating and frequent exercise are the secrets to keeping the body healthy and therefore increasing happiness.

It is scientifically proven that humans in shape are more jovial, in better spirits than those who do not exercise as much. Meet a grouch, and for sure he/she is not athletic. One cannot be in good humor without being in a healthy body. A buoyant body is a requirement for an upbeat mind.

Do not play much golf. It takes too much time away from your family, other things. So it's ok to play time-consuming sports only if your wife also has a major, time-consuming hobby, or if you do it with your children (or I guess with good friends if no children are around).

Save your body from injury. Before the age of 25, the highest chance of dying you have is through some accident. Motorcycles claim too many young lives. American football can break your bones, and even your brain through concussions. Choose your activities wisely.

<u>You must sweat for exercise to be good</u>. I actually adore the feeling of drips of sweat on my forehead. I even relish the sensation of it evaporating off my skin and cooling me off. I do not like it when Paola caringly would want to wipe it off my skin. Science says the heartbeat must increase significantly to be able to burn fat. To get the most regeneration from exercise.

<u>In general, team sports are more fun</u>. Soccer, basketball, volleyball, waterpolo, are all sports I have a lot of fun playing. It's like getting 2 for the price of 1. Needed exercise, and positive interaction with friends. Most activities in your life are best done together.

<u>Swimming will give you the broadest shoulders</u>. It is the one complete sport, where every muscle of your body gets flexed, used, burned. It will shape your body to be desirable, not only to feel good.

<u>Eating is one of the most delightful activities in life</u>. This is one of the many situations where 'In medio stat virtus' is the maxim to follow. Enjoy eating, but in moderation. You cannot enjoy good health, you cannot feel well, if you eat excessively. We are in a moment in the history of the world where many have too much to eat.

<u>It's what you eat that really counts</u>. One of the secrets is to enjoy feeling thin. Good taste in your mouth is certainly pleasurable, but it's very short lived. You have to concentrate on how good it feels to be in shape, to have a flat belly, to be able to run somewhere and not be out of shape.

<u>Once you concentrate on this feeling of vigor and wellness, you'll be able to stop eating as soon as you are full</u>. To appreciate when you are eating only for the taste, not because your body is hungry. Feeling a bit of hunger before every meal is a good feeling, one our modern society has forgotten.

Do not eat too much at night. You will be able to metabolize a heavy lunch (which you should not have either). But lots of calories at dinner, and then straight to bed, will force your body to store as fat most of the calories. This is one of the reasons, I believe, for the obesity epidemic. Have a light meal for supper, and have it at least 3 hours before lying down for your 8 hours of sleep.

Sleep about 8 hours, regularly. It is well proven scientifically that lack of rest causes our organism to crave sweets. After a night 'on call', having slept less than 4-5 hours, I feel the need to eat continuously. Especially high-glucose foods. I 'feel' I'm getting fat. If I sleep all night, and have my usual cereals with soy milk, I feel great.

In a fat body a mind slips and slides everywhere. Pay a lot of attention to what you eat. In the past, our ancestors needed to care most about getting something to eat. Now food is in abundance in our developed societies. So we should care most about what we eat. We should count calories, and decide what amounts of protein, carbohydrates, and fat are best for each of us.

Money

Money can buy a house,
But not a family.

Money can buy a watch,
But not time.

Money can buy a bed,
But not good sleep.

Money can buy a book,
but not knowledge.

Money can pay a doctor,
but not acquire health.

Money can buy you a position,
But not respect.

Money can buy blood,
But not life.

Money can buy sex,
But not love.

Chinese proverb

Money is certainly important, but <u>some of the most essential things in life cannot be bought</u>. You need to work towards achieving them with means other than money. Usually with your good will, amiability, and commitment.

<u>What counts in life is what you earn</u>. Not what you inherit from relatives. Do not rely on what you might get as donations. Obtaining financial security is up to you, not your family, friends, spouse, or others.

<u>Your parents should provide you with an education, affection, love, sane principles</u>, like the ones in this book. These are more essential than to give you wealth. Parents can protect their kids a lot more by being examples of rectitude, than with money.

I agree with Bill Gates: <u>inheriting too much money will spoil children</u>. It robs them of their incentive to do something in life. Of his over $50 billion (maybe more now), each of his daughters is getting about $10 million. A lot of money, but less than 0.1% of what they could have gotten. An amount sufficient enough to have a comfortable life, but not one that can allow lavish laziness.

Fortunately or unfortunately, depending how you see it, your mother and I do not even have such millions to pass along. We hope to pay for your education, as our parents did for us, and to provide financial security. You'll want to, and have to, make your own money to pass the same to your children.

<u>Be prudent with your money</u>. Do not be stingy, but be aware that every penny saved is a penny made. <u>Before buying something</u>, think how you will feel tomorrow about it. Are you just seeking to buy for the trill of the acquisition? For the short-lived pleasure of possession? Or do you really need, and will use for a long time, what you are buying? The best things in life <u>aren't things</u>.

<u>Save as much as feasible</u>. Every month, put some money aside in a different bank account that you will not touch for spending. Even if it's a few dollars. And begin doing it when you are in your twenties, with your first pay-checks.

<u>Invest in something solid, like a house, an apartment, a piece of land</u>. My maternal grandfather had a small stipend working in a bank. Nonetheless he was able, over the course of a lifetime, to buy several small apartments, often by first mortgaging them. He was able to pass them along to his two daughters, my mother and her sister. Thanks to his dedication and financial acumen in real estate, my mother and her sister never had to work, always being secure with small rents of his investments.

Do not spend much money on fancy cars, or clothes, or jewelry. I was lucky my wife Paola told me after the first 10 years of marriage that she had way too much jewelry, and she did not want anymore. Great! What a smart co-pilot! She knows we can save that money for something more valuable long-term to the 4 of us.

Be aware that often behind a big sudden fortune, there is a crime, as said by Honore' de Balzac. Almost always, it takes a while to make money, and accumulate wealth. Do it honestly. It will make you feel good. Fancy schemes, gambling, promises of quick riches, often will lead to ruin.

Religion

The true nature of things, that we shall never know, never.
Albert Einstein

<u>I feel there is God given my sense of wonder of the world.</u> My sense of many things being inexplicable, incomprehensible. I can believe in God not because of proof that he exists. My explanation for my faith in God is that I cannot explain it. God is so much 'above' us in comprehension that we cannot grasp its full significance. This is my religion.

<u>God for me is you, me, the earth, plants, animals, this desk, everything.</u> He is everything. I cannot even define him. He is way out of my league. I venerate the intangible, the inexplicable, the force behind what I can understand.

<u>I am a scientist, but the true meaning of certain things escapes our intellect.</u> Can you describe Beethoven's 5th symphony as a variation of wave pressure? Yes. But it's a description which does not give you the true meaning of this magnificent symphony. As I enjoy this music, I even more, incomprehensibly more, benefit from the thought of God being in and all around me.

I remember vividly my discussions on these topics with my good friend Pierluigi while we were in high school. We were the best students in our class, but he was the hardened communistic, a fervent atheist. The son of a philosopher, and a great mind and convincing speaker himself, he was hard to convince, not matter what the topic. He always could quote from famous logicians, and undo my arguments.

While walking on the beach of our hometown of Pescara, on the Adriatic sea, we discussed of life, love, death, religion, and the meaning of it all. I am still impressed by my own reasoning on religion then, as he admitted that my way of believing in God as something that cannot be explained by man was indeed valid. In a way, he reinforced my faith.

<u>All I know is that God loves me a lot</u>. He is a friend I can always count on. I do not ask him much. He has given me so much, so much joy, every day, that I just thank him continuously. He is inside me, so I can reveal my feelings to him without fear. I can hear his voice advising me, pointing me in the right direction.

<u>I think science and God are completely compatible</u>. I believe in Darwinian evolution. I believe in the Big Bang. And perhaps before the Big Bang there were many more such, or similar, events. That still begs the questions: what was before the primordial Big Bang? Who is responsible for that?

<u>I'm sure we'll come up with more scientific discoveries, that we'll find out what was before the Big Bang, but still the question will remain. Who?</u> Who was responsible for all this? Who started it all? As our minds get lost in the incomprehensible, that's where I find my God.

<u>God is different than religion</u>. Do not confuse the two. God made God (again, incomprehensible). Humans made the church and religion. That is why I prefer God to religion. Unfortunately many, too many, in fact millions of people, have died because of religion.

<u>Do not follow religion too closely</u>. Especially do not become a fanatical of just 'your' religion. Who says Islam is better than Judaism, or Christianity, or Buddhism, or any other religion? Believing that your chosen religion is the only true one is to me nonsense.

<u>A bit of history and some common wisdom</u> says we cannot seriously think we know much about God. I do not want to oversimplify facts that have been studied for centuries and examined in thousands of books. And I apologize for any possible mistakes. But some facts must be known. Facts, not opinions. Be open to the truth, even when talking about religion.

<u>Have you ever heard of the Crusades?</u> These are the quintessential wars of religion. The Crusades were 9 wars, lasting about 200 years, of Christians mainly against Muslims, but also against pagan Slavs, pagan Balts, Jews, Russian and Greek

Orthodox Christians, Mongols, Cathars, Hussites, Waldensians, Old Prussians, and political enemies of the Popes. The Popes did not conquer back their Holy Land, but in fact only caused the unnecessary deaths of thousands of knights, and of many faithful innocents.

<u>Unfortunately too many other wars have been waged because of religion</u>. Both in antiquity, as well as today. In fact history has repeated itself many times, and the list of wars of religion is certainly too long for me to condense it in this small chapter. Even modern wars of the West, involving also the US, such as the one against Iraq, have some religious motives and implications.

<u>Christianity came about only because a small group of Israelites believed that Jesus was God reincarnated, while most did not</u>. There were initially no other differences. Certainly the books we follow are similar, except again for the stories about Jesus, i.e. the Gospel. But there are many more similarities than differences.

<u>Anglicanism</u> came about because Henry the VIII wanted to get married and divorced as many times as he pleased, without asking permission from the Pope. There is nothing elegiac about his story, except the fact that divorce is a fact of life, and should indeed be allowed.

<u>I grew up Catholic, being taught that Martin Luther 'divided' the church</u>. Again here a dispassionate study of history helps to clarify. The Roman Church was asking for money from sinners to absolve their transgressions. Luther's main belief was that God can directly, without any intercession by the Church, declare a sinner righteous. Deliverance could be obtained, as it is taught in the Sacred Scriptures, by faith alone through God's grace. So the Church was corrupt to exploit its power and ask for money, often from very poor people, to redeem the people's sins. This does not seem to me so bad, now that I can reflect on these facts with an adult intellect.

<u>The Catholic Church has made several other significant mistakes in its 2,000-year-old history</u>. I cannot comprehend how they can be against contraception, which saves lives. How can they

be against condoms, even when they protect against potentially fatal illnesses such as HIV? How they can be against pre-marital sex, which allows two people who will stay together hopefully for the rest of their life to really test their compatibility? How can they not allow more than half of humanity, women, to become priests and therefore representatives of God? In the twenty-first century, the wisdom of the world, scientific and non-scientific, has surpassed these old myths.

But there are also many good things about religion. All religions have the same basic teachings. The commandments are about the same in all religions. They are 'ancient and proven truths' which humanity has come to universally agree on. Homo sapiens, who evolved from earlier hominids about 20,000 years ago, began to develop some of these a long time ago.

These old and true principles are derived by millennia of human thinking. They are the product of wisdom tested by time and passed on for hundreds of generations. So follow these basic, well accepted, commandments. To me they have to be put into today's social context. Check out the commandments from different religions:

The Jewish and Christian (Catholic, Lutheran, Anglican, Orthodox, Reformed, etc) faiths have the same famous 10 commandments (as reported twice in Exodus, and in Deuteronomy):

1. I am the Lord your God; You shall have no other Gods before me;
2. You shall not make for yourself an idol;
3. You shall not make wrongful use of the name of your God;
4. Remember the Sabbath and keep it holy;
5. Honor your father and mother;
6. You shall not murder;
7. You shall not commit adultery;
8. You shall not steal;
9. You shall not bear false witness against your neighbor;

10. You shall not covet your neighbor's wife (or anything that belongs to your neighbor).

I want to again emphasize these are the SAME for these two apparently so different religions. Jews and Christians have fought for 2 millennia despite the same basic principles. In fact, you could say that the sacred scriptures are for the most part the same for each of these major religions. I'd like to comment on each of these commandments.

1. *I am the Lord your God; you shall have no other Gods before me.* I must admit I have a little problem with this one. Who is God? As I said, God to me is the incomprehensible. He is everything. So how can we have 'no other Gods'? He is already the only one by definition, as he is everything. He would have no need to distinguish himself from anything. Saying 'you shall have no other Gods before me' is certainly an erroneous human interpretation. My rationalization is that early followers of a particular religion wanted to say their beliefs (and therefore their God) were superior to those of others. Unnecessary wars have been fought because of this 'you shall have no other Gods before me'. It would be acceptable maybe to say that 'you shall have nothing before me'. This would mean that a person, or food, or place, or whatever else, could not be more important than God. I would understand that. Instead 'No other Gods before me' means also that you should stay away from other religions. I can tell you you'll learn a lot from other religions and from their followers. And that the 'Gods' over 90% of people follow are just about the same.

2. *You shall not make for yourself an idol.* Worshiping icons is just wrong. If a statue represents God for you, it's ok to pray to it. But it is not the statue you ought to adore; it is the idea of God. Again, irrational battles

have been fought to regain an icon. Even the desolate and penniless can have God.
3. *You shall not make wrongful use of the name of your God.* Respect is one of my essential credos. God demands the highest deference. Cursing God is not excusable. But I do not think it will get someone to hell (which I'm not sure exists as described by Christianity).
4. *Remember the Sabbath and keep it holy.* This is one issue that has extreme actuality. In our busy lives, packed with events, we forget to stop and think. We forget, most sinfully, to thank (someone) for our blessings. We do not pause to review the events of the last week, and ponder on those in the near and far future. Meditation is beneficial, and revered in all religions.

This commandment also reminds me of the points I made in the chapters 'Work hard' and 'Play hard'. If you have done your duties during the week, you certainly deserve at least a day to recuperate. In fact, if you do not take some time off work, you will be less productive the following week.

Last, this commandment reminds me of the foolishness of man. The Jewish faith celebrates the 'Sabbath' on Saturday, in fact starting Friday at dusk until Saturday at dusk. The Christians have taken Sunday as their holy day. This happened after the Jewish-Roman wars of the 1st and 2nd centuries, and then of 351 and finally of 613. Oppositions to Judaism by Romans and Christian clergy led them to despise the Sabbath, so they moved the day of worship to Sunday. Many Christian groups never agreed, and still keep the Sabbath as Holy day.

Being the number 1 religion for most of recent history (lately Islam became the most popular), Christianity has made Sunday a vacation day for most

humans, and Monday the standard start of the working week.
5. *Honor your father and mother.* As a father, this is one I certainly approve of. It is also a commandment I tried to comply with as a child towards my own parents. Now that I have been both a son and a father, I appreciate even more the wisdom of this ancient principle.

   Your mother and father have something you do not and cannot have more than them, ever. They have experience. They have 20, 30 more years of life than you. You might indeed be smarter than them. And you certainly may see things differently than them. But their opinion is based on having been in similar situations often many times, having studied, having read books, having traveled, having thought often long and hard about the issue you just want to make a decision on based on your naïve intuition. Respect their opinions, the help they want to provide, and indeed their whole persona. Remember these two individuals are your biggest allies. They might treat you as you treat them if you antagonize them. Make them your most cherished allies, and hold them in high regard.
6. *You shall not murder.* This is basic and self-explanatory. And I could end it here. The Christians prefer the word 'kill' to 'murder' compared to Jews. Life is sacred, and should not be taken by one man from another. I do believe that killing in battle is murder. I am against capital punishment. Even the rare evil persons, who certainly exist, should just be kept in jail for life, with continuous attempts to improve them and make them contributors to the wellness of others. Our Darwinian evolution has taken us at least to this level. 'A tooth for a tooth,' or 'An eye for an eye' are ancient,

unethical and even sinful sayings, more appropriate for beasts than for 21st century humans.
7. *You shall not commit adultery*. This goes back to the 'Girls' and especially 'Life-long partner' chapters. Marriage means being committed and faithful to someone else, and only that person, for life. So going out with 10 girls at the same time seems not to be a sin, as long as neither you nor any of them are married. Not that this is behavior you should seek. But the point here is that, if and when you decide to swear, officially, your loyalty to a spouse, then you should adhere to your commitment. Monogamy is what religion demands.

But is it religion? Once again, I believe religion just followed common universal wisdom. Life is best lived in two, and any long-lasting and solid relationship should be based on mutual admiration, honesty, sincerity, and respect. No extra-marital affairs. No cheating allowed. Marriage is a serious endeavor, a life-commitment, with all its positive and less positive aspects.
8. *You shall not steal*. This is another obvious commandment. But, while murder is pretty rare, I believe stealing is commonplace. Not just robbing banks. Or shoplifting. To me not paying taxes is stealing. Taking a job that someone else rightfully deserves more than you, is stealing. Appropriating for our own glory someone else's idea or discovery is robbing.
9. *You shall not bear false witness against your neighbor*. This also goes back to my Universal Commandments chapter. Honesty and sincerity are basic principles, and should be laws of life which should be automatically and universally part of every behavior. Being deceitful against anyone, anytime, is inexcusable. I do believe it

should not be tolerated, and should be appropriately condemned.
10. *You shall not covet your neighbor's wife* (or anything that belongs to your neighbor). This must have been a major issue, as commandment #7 covers a similar topic. It's interesting to me how obviously this problem must have been present for humanity for a long time. In fact, even little knowledge of animal life tells us this is an issue that often ends in bloodshed in other lesser species. So we have created a rule to avoid this kind of conflict, trying to keep couples together. In general, this is a directive to follow. As there are, as I said earlier, over 1 billion possible companions, one who is already married should not be the one you seek. Especially if they are your neighbor, or friend. And everyone could be your neighbor or friend.

While Islam teaches that the texts of the Torah and the Gospels have been corrupted from their divine originals over the years, messages from these holy books of the Jews and Christians still coincide closely with certain verses in Islam's holy book, the Qur'an (Koran):

1. *"There is no other god beside God."* (Qur'an 47:19)
2. *"My Lord, make this a peaceful land, and protect me and my children from worshiping idols."* (Qur'an 14:35)
3. *"And make not Allah's (name) an excuse in your oaths against doing good, or acting rightly, or making peace between persons; for Allah is One Who heareth and knoweth all things."* (Qur'an 2:224) This quranic verse is not entirely analogous to the Old Testament's, but the similarity is evident.
4. *"O you who believe, when the Congregational Prayer (Salat Al-Jumu`ah) is announced on Friday, you shall hasten to the commemoration of God, and drop all business."*

(Qur'an 62:9) According to the teachings of Islam, the Sabbath was abrogated by the revelation of Muhammed. Furthermore, the Sabbath was only decreed for the Jews. (Qur'an 16:124) I wonder if these seemingly arbitrary changes were made just to distinguish a new religion from the old. In fact, the Islamic story goes that God ordered Muslims to make every effort to drop all business to attend the congregational (Friday) prayer. The more in depth one looks at these differences, the more one understand many changes were certainly subjective, and should not give rise to resentment or disputes.

5. *"....and your parents shall be honoured. As long as one or both of them live, you shall never (even) say to them, "Uff" (the slightest gesture of annoyance), nor shall you shout at them; you shall treat them amicably."* (Qur'an 17:23) It's interesting how the Qur'an, written thousands of years after the Bible or Torah, is often giving the same wisdom, but being more explanatory.

6. *"....anyone who murders any person who had not committed murder or horrendous crimes, it shall be as if he murdered all the people."* (Qur'an 5:32) Here again the Qur'an seems stricter, with zero tolerance.

7. *"You shall not commit adultery; it is a gross sin, and an evil behaviour."* (Qur'an 17:32) Again, this basic concept of avoiding extramarital sex, especially of a married woman with a man who is not her husband, is thousands of years old. It was then codified by the Judeo-Christian doctrines, and is even present as a concept in Hinduism.

8. *"They shall not steal."* (Al-Mumtahanah 60: 12) Exactly the same. Except that Islam here takes one more, big step: *"The thief, male or female, you shall cut off their hands as a punishment for their crime, and to serve as an example from God. God is Almighty, Most Wise."* (Qur'an 5:38) I think even most Muslims understand that this was an exaggeration linked to the tough times in which these phrases were written,

i.e. the Middle Ages. Just as capital punishment should be banned, physical injury should also be left to past history.
9. *"Do not withhold any testimony by concealing what you had witnessed. Anyone who withholds a testimony is sinful at heart."* (Qur'an 2:283)
10. *"And do not covet what we bestowed upon any other people. Such are temporary ornaments of this life, whereby we put them to the test. What your Lord provides for you is far better, and everlasting."* (Qur'an 20:131)

I'm not going to make this a book about religion, but many other cultures and faiths have similar principles. The Egyptians commandments written on the temples along the Nile were almost identical to the ones we just reviewed. Hinduism, Buddhism, and many other religions have as their basis similar teachings, accepted in almost all cultures and societies.

Since I was a teenager, I have this conviction that differing religions were made by humans who wanted followers and therefore power. I do not see the need to split in front of God because one believes in 'eating the body of Christ' and others do not (but still use leavened bread).

There are some great priests. They are the ones that show most their humanity. The ones who have had girlfriends, who have had sex, who have lived a life before putting the vest on. The ones who know and appreciate other faiths. True scholars of God should know and be familiar with all creeds. Should work to reconcile differences and enhance similarities. They know that all monotheistic major religions have some benefits to humans. That divisions are destructive. They are true pastors of souls towards a common, all-loving, universal and incomprehensible God.

I guess my true creed is the universal commandments I describe earlier in this book. I mention many more than in other doctrines. I think that, a few hundred years since the latest major new faith, humanity has acquired more wisdom. But it still has major problems applying most of this good judgment.

<u>I can worship and thank God in any synagogue, temple, or church</u>. These are all great places to meditate, if you have been in one. Treating others as I would like to be treated, is part of my religion. Working and playing hard. Being honest, sincere, and trying to better not just my future, but also the world's, and everyone else's. These principles belong in all places of faith.

<u>It's scientifically proven that believing in God, praying, and meditating, improves your health, and makes you live longer</u>. I love to kneel in church, and thank God for all I was given. Places of worship are wonderful for reflecting on one's life and blessings. Poorly lighted, quiet, often a bit cold, so you often have to keep your coat on, they offer the opportunity to look inside oneself, and find God, or whatever you want to call 'the inexplicable' of existence. Kneeling down makes you concentrate on yourself, the brain closer to the heart as you bow down, back almost in fetal position, as you were first made.

<u>It's good to pray if that makes us stronger</u>, helping us to believe in ourselves more. Remedies lie within ourselves, and yearning for improvement does make us stronger. <u>But do not expect somebody in the sky to come down and do it for you</u>. That 'someone' will look over your shoulder and guide you, but it's still you who has to do what Heaven will direct you to.

Country

Ask not what America will do for you, but what together we can do for the freedom of man.
John Fitzgerald Kennedy

<u>It does not matter where you live. It's important how you live.</u> If you follow the advice from this book, you can live in Peking, or Rome, or the Amazon: anywhere you'll have a good life.

<u>Be aware there is no perfect place</u>. But some places are better for you than others. I like the beach, and missed it living in Philadelphia and New York. But I willingly sacrificed looking at the Adriatic for better professional gratification.

<u>My first time in Denmark</u>, I had to take a taxi from the train station to the resort hotel where the international conference I was speaking at was being held. I conversed for about 20 minutes with the friendly taxi driver. He told me:

"Nothing happens here. Everybody is nice, polite, there is hardly any crime. In fact, it's boring. So, every year I take one week in which I travel outside of Denmark. Once I'm out, I discover that other countries are often dirty, disorganized; that the state does not help its citizens; that there is more poverty, less public assistance; that people are less honest, and that there is more crime. So, at the end of the week, I come back home, and learn again to love the 'boredom' of efficiency and safety of Denmark."

This story reminds me that the grass is not always greener on the other side. Learn to appreciate what you have. <u>Every place has its pluses and minuses</u>. Often we forget the advantages of where we live, and dream of how much better life could be in.... Be careful.

While you are both American and Italian by birth, <u>do not have any special attachment to any state or national entity whatsoever</u>. These two are places that will always remind you of your youth and your culture, but the world should be your playground.

In fact, even national flags should not be revered as much as they are. They are symbols of separations, and there's an army behind almost every flag. I salute the world flag; humanity as one global flag. Patriotism should not imply hating other states.

There probably should not be any independent countries. Only one world. John Lennon imagined 'all the people, living life in peace.' No borders. As long as you respect common laws, you are free. Foster the ability of all people, of all kinds, to live together, in the same world, in harmony with each other.

Do not go to war. Do not enlist in the military. The killing of human beings in a war is no better than common murder (as said by Albert Einstein). Weapons attract violence. Keeping a weapon at home only increases the chance you'll be killed. It's proven scientifically.

Be against the death penalty. Every human being should have the chance to redeem himself, and become a better person. I have never seen scientific proof that the death penalty is a deterrent against crime.

Be open to people of other nationalities. Just like you, every being is a unique manifestation of the human spirit. I'm so happy you already have Chinese, black, Vietnamese, Algerian, Peruvian, Irish, Spanish friends. They will each teach you something new of their culture, and allow you to understand the world better.

These relationships will make you also a better person, since you'll be able to pick out something from each of the different cultures, choosing whatever best fits your personality and your beliefs.

Based on these principles, when you want to do something good, make sure it's good for everyone, not just for one nation. And don't demand, but give: JF Kennedy said in 1961 that you should "ask not what America will do for you, but what together we can do for the freedom of man." I love this concept.

<u>See the world. Traveling will open your mind</u>. Traveling will allow you to compare different ways to live. It will teach you that the way you were always taught to do things is not always right. It will make you appreciate Muslims, Jews, Christians, Buddhists, Hindus, all religions, all beliefs. Studying these, you'll discover that they all have goodness in them, that they are all good. You can pick up good from all beliefs, all people, all paths of life, all nations.

<u>The world is complex, and traveling lets you understand it better</u>. The world is a book, and you do not want to read just one page. <u>Often people distrust what they do not know</u>. People despise what they have not seen before, what is foreign. <u>Make sure nothing is foreign to you, so you can judge it not for its color or appearance, but for its values.</u>

Count on me

"Boys and their fathers don't always have much to say to each other unless and until they trust."
Barack Obama

<u>Count on me</u>. You can trust me. As I'd like to trust you. And count on you. You are my son. I do not expect that you become a king or a champion. But I hope you'll try to always do your best. As I have tried to.

<u>You know that you can find refuge, unconditional love, and even emergency funds in the house of your mother and father</u>. This is what family is for. Trust on us as your shelter. As the safe haven you can always come to and relax in. The shoulder where you can cry on. The embrace that will always embrace you back, no matter what. The endless love that will always love you back. The bank where there is always some money.

<u>I know that you have already learned the lessons in these pages</u>. I already know that if I fall asleep for a long time you can manage well. You already have the character and virtues I wanted you to embrace. I am leaving these lines as a reminder, and maybe to help the generations after yours.

<u>Also count on me fading away</u>. I do not want to be overbearing in your life. Too many children are ruined by their parents. I have passed on the will to excel, the taste for success. But I do not want to be too big a myth of a parent. I did my thing, of which I'm proud. You do not have to do the same thing, you just have to do something you'll be proud of when you are over 40.

<u>The world is yours. Go and conquer life your way</u>. Do not be afraid to enter a contest, but face with serenity your challenges. "I did it my way", as Frank Sinatra said in his beautiful song "My way", written by Paul Anka and first recorded in 1969, is good advice. Once you are assured of my love and your mother's love, forget us for a while, and go on exploring the world. Conquer your little space in the sun.

But remember to call us to join in your celebrations!

Conclusion

He who dies with the most good deeds, wins.

These are the basic lessons I understood in life. For me, some of the most essential were finding a wonderful wife to share life with; having two great sons to have fun with; working to the best of my abilities, passionately, to save and improve lives of mothers and babies; respecting and helping my parents; being a good example to others, for honesty, hard work, niceness; teaching and writing books that can help others, both in medicine and in life; being able to sleep well at night, with no regrets.

Be better than me. You have the advantage of seeing my defects. The Chairman of Ob-Gyn at Cornell University and New York Hospital narrated to me once a telling story. He admits he has battled with his weight most of his adult life. He then was surprised none of his kids are overweight, and indeed they are skinny. Then someone told him that they probably learned to stay fit from seeing their father's struggles, and wanted to improve compared to him. Follow this kind of example.

You will have to make your own successes, go through your own mistakes. The beautiful thing is, you define what success is for yourself. Aim high. Do not settle for modesty or the shadows of inertia. Leave a mark. Often success comes to those that are so dedicated to good causes that they are too busy looking for success.

Do not let fame be mistaken for success. How many famous people merit your admiration? Few, if any. Success is not money, either. Success is giving more than receiving. Success is being proud to improve the health and life of an individual. To enhance humanity.

In the end, what counts is your judgment of yourself. What was important in your life to you is what matters. From the outside, people may have liked you because of broad shoulders, or because you helped them pass an exam. Their judgment is secondary compared to what you think of yourself.

Being happy does not mean everything is perfect. It means you can see beyond the imperfection. Being happy means you like what you do. You do it with purpose, with joy. Strive to understand what makes you happy, and avoid whatever hurts you.

Later in life, and even in the middle of it, you'll want to assess how things are going for yourself. Much satisfaction comes from looking back and seeing that you have devoted your efforts to good causes. That you have improved the world. That you have enhanced the lives, the health, the minds, of many. Or even few, but those few have had significant benefit from your example, from your energy for improvement towards good.

I'm still afraid of flying. So every time I'm up above the clouds at 30,000 feet, I feel inside the sensation that I might soon die. That I might be living the last moments of my life. So I consider my life. And I'm happy, I know I would die content, having already accomplished in life the main goals I wanted to achieve.

Happiness is a trip that starts when you are young. I hope you have started the trip on the right foot. Whatever it takes, I want to hear Pietro always sing in his carefree happiness, and Andrea smile with his cute eyes and mouth.

December 13, 1997

Ciao Andrea,
you know, my 'bellissimo', that you celebrate your 13th day of life today? Now you are near me, close to my desk. We are waiting for mom Paola to come back, so she can feed you the milk you like so much. You and her are currently inseparable. You scream. It looks to me you're very hungry. Just wait for your mother, you know I cannot give you your favorite milk!

You are so well behaved, that's it, pacifier and silence. You do not demand much. You sleep, ask for food when hungry, then eat voraciously like all your predecessors. Poop and 'pipi', often and happily, burps and super-burps, an occasional fart while your grandmother Luigia holds you…You are the perfect neonate, no question about it.

You are warm, soft, smoother than worn-out cotton, or velvet. You allow yourself to be kissed by our overpowering and humid love. But as long as there's food to eat and a warm little sleeping place, you are fine. You do not care much about light, others moving around, noises. You sleep, eat, that's all.

It's splendid having you in my arms. You smell like maternal milk, a scent I was not familiar with before. It's sugary, warm, a pheromone. I had tried to imagine this sensation of embracing you in my arms or holding you towards the sky many times. The pride of being a father. I discover myself less selfish. I find again my passionate love for life. Too many say the world is unpleasant, that it must be changed. Well, I'm having a great time, and wish the same to you.

I imagine your happiness while playing with your toys, cars, miniature soccer players. Your joy while having fun with your friends at school. I can picture you now after school running towards your mom or me for a hug. I can envision your cheerful sweating during the first tennis game, a soccer match, all the sports I hope I can teach you. I can foresee the pleasure you'll have licking a gelato, swimming in the sea, the first rendezvous with girls, the first courting, the first kisses…

I wish you a wonderful life. Squeezing you gently in my arms, I hope to help you achieve your great potential without interfering excessively. I'll be your guardian angel. Just from behind the scene.

Acknowledgements

Andy Hallmann
Paola Luzi
Tim Rafael
Jay Goldberg
Andrea Berghella

www.ingramcontent.com/pod-product-compliance
Lightning Source LLC
Chambersburg PA
CBHW020012050426
42450CB00005B/439